The Lone Samurai
and the Martial Arts

The Lone Samurai
and the Martial Arts

Stephen Turnbull

ARMS AND
ARMOUR

◀ **The defiant lone samurai** A print by Yoshitoshi
showing one of the reactionary samurai of the Restoration
Wars. (Courtesy of the Oranda-jin Gallery, the
Netherlands)

Dedicated to my son Alex,
without whom this book would never have been written . . .

First published in Great Britain in 1990 by Arms and Armour Press,
Artillery House, Artillery Row, London SW1P 1RT.

Distributed in the USA by Sterling Publishing Co. Inc.,
387 Park Avenue South, New York, NY 10016-8810.

Distributed in Australia by Capricorn Link (Australia) Pty. Ltd,
P.O. Box 665, Lane Cove, New South Wales 2066, Australia.

British Library Cataloguing in Publication Data
Turnbull, Stephen
The lone Samurai and the martial arts.
1. Samurai. Japan, history
I. Title
305.5'2
ISBN 0-85368-967-9

Jacket illustrations: Front, a 6th *Dan* in the martial art of *Kendō*,
wearing modern *Kendō* armour and holding a bamboo *shinai* —
equipment that has changed little in the past two centuries. (Photograph
by Michael Dyer Associates). Back, a print by Kunisada of an actor as
the Swordsman Miyāmoto Musashi. He has been attacked in a bath-
house and is wearing a *yukata* (bath-robe); his valuables are in a pouch
hanging from his neck.

Designed and edited by DAG Publications Ltd. Designed by
David Gibbons; edited by Michael Boxall; layout by Anthony A. Evans;
typeset by Typesetters (Birmingham) Ltd, Warley; camerawork by
M&E Reproductions, North Fambridge, Essex; printed and bound in
Great Britain by Courier International Ltd, Tiptree, Essex.

Contents

Introduction

The figure approaches from a distance, following the dusty road over the brow of a hill. As he gets closer he is seen to have the appearance of a man, travel-stained and wild, and a sword is at his side. He stops, and our eyes meet. Another man is nearby. He too is armed, and he is waiting. The opponents approach each other. There is the flash of a swordblade . . .

This is the image projected almost daily by a million television screens, comics and films. The wanderer is victorious, and he will wander again. He is an expert in the martial arts, ruthless and deadly, and always ready for his next encounter. He is the lone samurai. This image is also fostered in the modern practice of the martial arts of Japan, whose devotees are heir to a great tradition. This tradition consists of the arts themselves, refined and modified in response to changing conditions, but also to the more subtle and esoteric tradition of the brave individual warrior.

All my previous books have tended to concentrate on the samurai as a member of an army, and I have argued many times in the past that the generals of the age of the samurai wars could not command an army of individuals. There had to be organization and delegation of responsibility, where the needs of individual glory had to be subordinated to the overall need to win the battle. A commander of those times, therefore, thought not in terms of samurai, but of samurai armies. All this is indeed true, but once the army had been moved into battle order like men on a chess board, and the bombardment of arrows, arquebus balls or cannon fire had subsided, the samurai army would be transformed into a mass of individual combats between spear and sword, sword and knife, knife and bare hands. This was the situation for which the samurai had been trained since boyhood, the moment for which all the ancestral legends reserved their proudest language.

Yet despite a long tradition of individual prowess, and the powerful image of the wandering swordsman, the lone samurai remains a figure of paradox in Japanese history. Both on and off the battlefield the development of Japanese society points to the supremacy of the group rather than of the individual. Japanese history, in fact, displays a tendency for groups to succeed, and indivi-

▶ A map of the pre-modern provinces of Japan, showing major lines of communication

INTRODUCTION

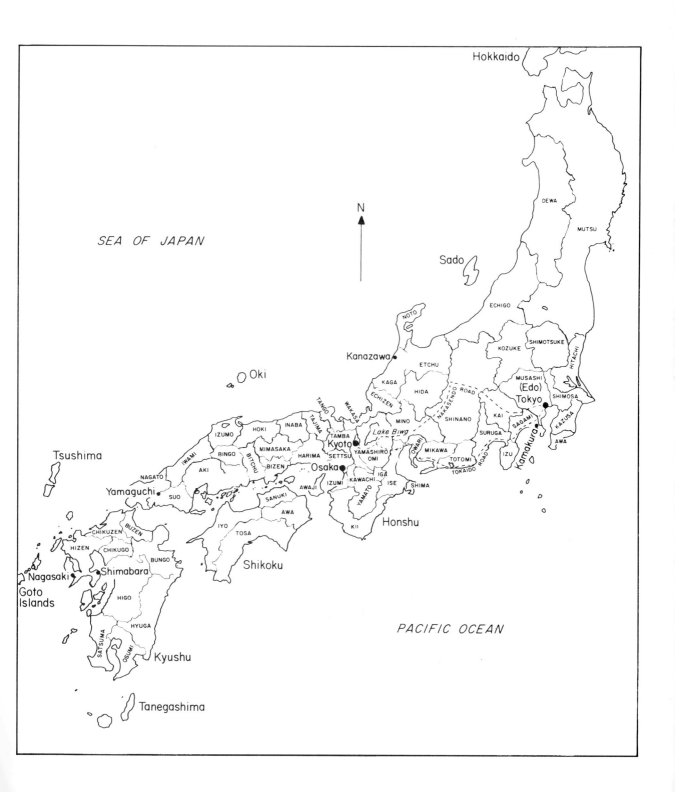

INTRODUCTION

duals to fail, which led Ivan Morris to entitle his study of the Japanese hero *The Nobility of Failure*, where he found a common thread of great endeavour being crushed, making the Japanese hero an eternally lonely and tragic figure.

We are therefore faced with two paradoxes. One is that the figure of the lone samurai, whose popularity is never in doubt throughout history, stands in direct contrast to what are perceived as the essentially group-led values of Japanese society. The other is that the hero figure with his destiny of doomed inevitability is contrary to that other popular perception of the Japanese people: their admiration for success, and their achievement of it.

In the pages which follow, therefore, I hope to set against Morris's 'nobility of failure' a wealth of examples of an even more prized 'nobility of success', as I examine this all-pervading tradition of the lone samurai. The resolution of the first paradox is less clear, for we shall see occasions when the desires of the individual warrior were clearly in conflict with the needs of the group. But there are other examples of a sensible and sensitive leader using this individual energy for the benefit of all, either as a brave warrior on the battlefield, as the sword instructor of the clan samurai, or as the wandering hero and deadly avenger of honour.

There is one other theme which we shall follow through these pages, and that is the development of the martial arts themselves, in particular those associated with single combat using sword, bow and spear. We shall see how their emphasis changes through history, and examine closely how these weapons were actually used in the time when skill meant survival, and failure, death.

This book has required a great deal of original research, and I should like to thank the numerous individuals who have supplied Japanese reference material and made many helpful suggestions, particularly Mr. Sadahiro Higuchi, of the Maniwa Nen-ryū, which preserves the old traditions of *kenjutsu*. Mrs. Nahoko Kitajima helped me very much on my visit to the sites described in these pages, and Shizue McGreavy helped me with the vast amount of translation that had to be done. I acknowledge the help of the staff of the libraries of Cambridge University, the School of Oriental and African Studies, London University, and the British Library. I also thank Terry O'Neill, the editor of *Fighting Arts International*. Some of the material which follows appeared first in this magazine in my series 'Samurai

Genesis'. I should also like to mention James Shortt, who has guided me through the early history of *jū-jutsu*, and once again Dunstan Gladthorpe has kindly allowed me to choose illustrations from his *Ehon Taikō-ki* to balance the modern view with that of old Japan. Several other private collections, which have asked not to be named, have provided other unique illustrative material. I am particularly grateful to *First Comics* of Chicago, for allowing me to use artwork from the English-language edition of the comic series *Lone Wolf and Cub*. I also acknowledge an art gallery in the Netherlands, the Oranda-jin, which kindly gave me photographs from past catalogues of the superb prints they sell.

Greatest thanks, as ever, are of course due to my dear wife Jo, and Alex, Richard and Katy, without whom nothing would be possible.

Stephen Turnbull, Leeds

Notes for the reader

Historical periods Japanese history of the time of the samurai is conveniently divided into a number of named periods, the names referring to the location of the imperial or Shogunal capital. The Heian Period, which includes the Gempei War, gives way to the Kamakura Period in 1192. With the fall of Kamakura in 1333 the capital shifted back to Kyōto and the Muromachi Period. The early Muromachi sees the Nambokuchō Wars, which finished in 1392. After the Ōnin War of 1467–7 the later Muromachi Period is usually referred to as the Sengoku Period, the 'Age of the Country at War'. The Sengoku includes the Momoyama Period from 1576, which continues until the coming of peace through the establishment of the Tokugawa Shogunate. The Tokugawa or Edo Period lasts from 1603 until 1868 and the Meiji Restoration.

Naming conventions Throughout this book the surname precedes the given name, except in the case of naming modern Japanese people. The suffixes -ji (temple), -yama (mountain) and -gawa (river) are used frequently where the context is clear.

1.

The Noble Samurai

The traditional image of the lone samurai is that of a wanderer, owing allegiance to none but himself and relying for his continued survival on his skills with the sword. This powerful picture is however a far cry from the reality of the earliest samurai warriors, who were aristocratic mounted archers, relying less on the sword than on the bow, and with their individual prowess in the martial arts the only feature they have in common with their later popular image.

The lone warrior in the age of the gods

The emergence of the samurai as the archetypal Japanese fighting man is preceded by many centuries of myth and legend, and Japan's long military tradition in fact goes back over two millenia. At the very beginning of time, according to the creation myths which explain the origins of the Japanese islands, we are faced with the image of a weapon. This first weapon is the coral spear which Izanagi, the father of the deities, plunges into the ocean, and from whose point drips water which coalesces into the land of Japan. Later in the same work (the *Kojiki, c.* AD 712) we see a reference to the most enduring Japanese martial image of all, when Izanagi uses a sword to kill the fire god, whose birth has led to the death of his wife Izanami.

Swords also play a part in the stories about the two surviving children of Izanagi: Susano-o, the thunder-god, and Amateratsu the goddess of the sun. The *Kojiki* tells us how Susano-o set off to destroy a monstrous serpent which was terrorizing the people. He hewed the serpent to pieces, but as he cut at its tail the blade of his sword was turned, and Susano-o discovered a finer sword buried therein. He called the sword *Ame no murakumo*, or 'cloud-cluster sword' from the dark clouds that clustered around the serpent, and presented it to his sister, who in turn gave it to her grandson who was to descend from heaven to rule the earth. This person's grandson who was Jimmu Tennō, the first Emperor of Japan, kept his sword as the first of the 'crown jewels' of the Japanese emperors.

Historical figures blend with the characters of mythology in the other early chronicle the *Nihon Shōki*, which gives us many details about the early emperors, to produce several individuals renowned for their prowess in the martial arts. Emperor Suizei, for example, the second ruler according to the traditional pedigree, was a

THE NOBLE SAMURAI

▲ **The Lone Samurai** The classic image of the lone samurai, fighting to the last against enormous odds. (from the *Ehon Taikō-ki*)

great expert in martial ways, as were several later crown princes. In AD 688 a certain Takata Iwanari was honoured by the incumbent Emperor Jitō for his success in the *san-hyō*, the three martial arts of bow, sword and spear.

The first lone warrior

It is not surprising to find that there are many elements of the lone samurai image, and martial arts lore, contained within the legend of the man who can be regarded as the first of the long line of brave individual warriors: Prince Yamato. 'Yamatotakeru-no mikoto', to give him his full title, is probably a composite character (Yamato is an ancient name for the Japanese nation), his exploits making a statement about the fierce struggles that were going on in Japan as the descendants of the 'sun-line' of emperors strove to assert the authority of their *uji*, or clan, against challengers.

The prince was the third son of the Emperor Keikō, and began his career inauspiciously when he murdered his elder brother. As a punishment he was dispatched to the island of Kyūshū, thus bringing in the element of a 'wandering swordsman' forced to head for a distant land where he might put his warrior skills to some positive use by opposing the enemies to the imperial line. Early on in Yamato's journey westwards we come across that most potent symbol of the Japanese warrior: the sword, for on his way he called in at the Great Shrine of Ise, where he was presented with the sword called *Ame no murakumo*, the 'cloud-cluster sword' which the deity Susano-o had wrested from the tail of the serpent. Armed with this miraculous weapon the hero set about his business of defeating the rebels.

It is fascinating to note how Yamato's first victory against a rebel chieftain is accomplished not solely by use of a sword, but by employing those skills which in later years would be listed under the techniques of *ninjutsu*, the arts of stealth and invisibility. Yamato's trick consisted of disguising himself as a woman with the sword 'cloud-cluster' concealed beneath his robes. He joined in with the merrymaking at the rebel leader's banquet, then at the right moment pounced on his victim.

The sword 'cloud-cluster' proved useful in another unconventional way some time later, when Prince Yamato was invited to join in a stag hunt near Mount Fuji, and realized very quickly that he was to be the quarry.

THE FIRST LONE WARRIOR

▲ **The first lone warrior** The legendary Prince Yamato is the first of a long line of individual warriors who meets a tragic death. In reality Yamato is probably a composite character (*Yamato* is an early name for Japan), but the tales of his exploits give a fascinating insight into the attitude of those early times. This statue of him is in the Kenroku-en gardens at Kanazawa. (From *Samurai Warriors*)

The hunters set fire to the long dry grass with the aim of either burning Yamato to death, or driving him in confusion towards their ambush. The Prince took the sword and cut his way through the burning grass to freedom, so that the sword 'cloud-cluster' became known as *Kusanagi*, the 'grass-mowing sword'. Here again is a powerful 'samurai' image: that of the warrior slashing wildly about him with his sword.

But a stranger enemy was lying in wait, in the shape of the monstrous serpent from whose tail the marvellous sword had been taken. On the first occasion of their meeting Prince Yamato had skipped unharmed over the beast, but on their second encounter the serpent got its revenge and stung Yamato in the heel, which brought on a fever. The Yamato legend concludes with his death from the fever, after which he was transformed into a white bird.

It is interesting to follow the Yamato legend just a little further, because the sword *Kusanagi* was the sacred sword of Japan, and with the mirror and the jewels is one of the three items of imperial regalia. It was deposited within the shrine of Atsuta, where the spirit of Prince Yamato was enshrined. In the appendix to the thirteenth-century epic, the *Heike Monogatari*, known as 'The Book of Swords', the anonymous author recounts another legend associated with the sacred sword. It concerns an attempt to steal the sword, and brings in a further element of martial accomplishment, namely unarmed combat. The thief was a Chinese priest called Dogyō who came to worship at the Atsuta Shrine and stayed for seven days, at the end of which he stole the sword, and wrapped it in the folds of his *kesa*, the priest's wide scarf-like garment. But the 'grass-mowing sword' had a will of its own, cut its way through the *kesa* and flew back to the shrine. Once more the priest took it, and wrapped it more securely, but again the sword made its escape. On his third attempt he managed to wrap the sword in nine folds of cloth, which was apparently sufficient to prevent it cutting its way through, and got away a considerable distance. At this point the enraged spirit of Prince Yamato sent a fellow *kami*, or deity, the Sumiyoshi Daimyōjin, to fight Dogyō for the sword. An interesting point about their subsequent combat is that victory was achieved by the deity kicking the thief to death, an early reminder that unarmed combat in Japan has always involved the use of *atemi*, decisive striking techniques with fist or foot.

This little-known fight, however, is not claimed as the first of its kind. Leaving aside an earlier combat between

THE NOBLE SAMURAI

▲ **Sumō in armour** An impromptu bout of *sumō* between two armoured warriors, from the *Ehon Taikō-ki*. *Sumō* is the oldest of the Japanese grappling arts, its origins lost in antiquity.

a deity and a mortal, which the deity won, an encounter in the presence of the Emperor Suinin, eleventh of the line, is often quoted as the origin of *sumō*, the traditional form of Japanese wrestling indelibly associated in the popular mind with the gargantuan professional champions of today. This innovatory fight was very different from *sumō* as we know it. According to the *Nihon Shōki* the victor won by delivering a kick from a standing position which broke his opponent's ribs and brought him to the ground. He then finished him off by trampling on him and breaking his hip bone.

The first samurai

To Prince Yamato, or to the actual warriors whose exploits provide the basis for the Yamato legend, the word *samurai*, which is often used to describe a Japanese

fighting man at any period, did not in fact exist. *Samurai* means 'one who serves', the service in question being military, and provided for a powerful overlord. The very appearance of the word indicates that an enormous change in the military and political life of Japan had taken place since the days of the early emperors. By the eighth century AD the emperor system had evolved from being a line of warrior chieftains, to whom prowess in the martial arts was a necessary fact of life, to a ruling house and lineage whose authority was effectively divine, through the descent the emperor could claim from the sun-goddess Amaterasu. Beneath the emperor was a bureaucracy, modelled on the civil service of China, and a conscript army built round the nucleus of an imperial guard.

But to some extent the nature of the imperial system was sowing the seeds, if not of its own destruction, then at least of its diminution in political terms. There were several factors in operation which made their mark over the next three centuries. First, there was a succession of younger imperial princes leaving the capital and heading off for the 'new frontiers' of Japan to serve their family's

THE FIRST SAMURAI

▶ **'The Way of Bow and Arrow'** A well-to-do samurai in everday clothes demonstrates his skill with a bow to a pair of admirers.

name and open up new territories, which may have strengthened the emperor's authority, but had the potential to weaken it by dispersal. Second, there was the domination of the imperial family by the Fujiwara clan, who supplied a seemingly endless line of consorts. This caused great jealousy among other powerful families who felt squeezed out. Two in particular greatly resented the Fujiwara domination. They were the *uji*, or clans of Taira and Minamoto, both of whom had imperial blood in their veins by courtesy of examples of the above-mentioned distant princes, and both of whom had built up spheres of influence far from the capital. The Taira were based in the west, on the shores of the Inland Sea, and the Minamoto to the east and north, where there were still *Ainu* tribes to fight. There were other great landowning families too, most of whom tended to ally themselves with one or other of the two power-blocs of Minamoto and Taira, but all had this in common: they were of unquestionable military skill, and although nominally owing allegiance to the distant emperor, their first loyalty was to their own family head, and the direction in which he would lead those 'who served' him – the samurai.

The emperors had the occasional rebels against the throne to deal with, and the frontiers of the civilized imperial state were constantly being pushed out at the expense of the aboriginal *Ainu* people. Both these tasks were performed eagerly by the samurai of the Taira and Minamoto, from which service they grew rich on rewards, and drew closer to the imperial court. So the centre held, and the 'sun-line' survived, as it has to this day, as the longest established ruling house in the world.

There was one other factor: the tendency that developed during the tenth century AD for an emperor to abdicate while still young and active in favour of a child

▶ **The Noble Samurai** This warrior is dressed in contemporary style for the Gempei Wars. His quiver of arrows is at his side, and he is about to fire an arrow with a broad U-shaped head. These were used for hunting, but may also have served to cut through the suspensory cords on a suit of armour.

relative, thus freeing him from the huge religious and ritual responsibility of kingship. There was thus produced a central figure who was still honoured, but who was also extremely vulnerable to manipulation. No rebel in Japan would ever have sought to overthrow the emperor. Such a course of action was unthinkable, and was also totally unnecessary. The important thing was to control the emperor, and it is these attempts by the Taira and the Minamoto to control emperors, or at least to control their nominees for the post, that forms the background to the civil wars which exploded during the twelfth century. Two minor skirmishes, called the *Hōgen* and *Heiji* 'disturbances' from the year names when they were fought, were superseded by a major war that lasted from 1180 to 1185 called the 'Gempei' War, from the Chinese reading of the names of Taira and Minamoto. After some initial success by the Taira their samurai were swept aside in a series of brilliant battles fought by the general Minamoto Yoshitsune, whose victories enabled his brother Yoritomo to become military dictator with a title that is almost as familiar as 'samurai', when Yoritomo became Japan's first *shōgun*. This set a pattern whereby Japan was to be dominated by the rule of the samurai for eight hundred years.

Samurai arms and armour

Before studying written accounts of samurai combat during this period let us first examine the context in which such combats were fought. The first point to note is that these contests were fought between men who were both armoured and mounted.

To begin with the armour. By the twelfth century the samurai were wearing armour of a characteristic design that was to have an important influence on the martial arts. It was made from small iron scales tied together and lacquered, then combined into armour plates by binding them together with silk or leather cords. This classic 'samurai armour' was therefore of lamellar construction (armour made from small plates fastened together) the traditional defensive armour of Asia, rather than the plate and mail of European knights. The standard 'suit of armour' of the classical samurai of the Gempei War was known as the *yoroi*. The body of the armour, the *dō*, was divided into four parts, giving the *yoroi* a characteristic box-like appearance. The two large shoulder plates, the *sode*, were fastened at the rear by the *agemaki*, a large ornamental bow. The *agemaki* allowed the arms fairly free movement while keeping the body always covered. Two guards were attached to the shoulder straps to prevent the tying cords from being cut, and a sheet of ornamented leather was fastened across the front to stop the bow string from catching on any projection.

The iron helmet bowl was commonly of 8–12 plates, fastened together with large projecting conical rivets, and the neck was protected with a heavy five-piece *shikoro*, or neckguard, which hung from the bowl. The top four plates were folded back at the front to form the *fukigayeshi*, which stopped downward cuts aimed at the horizontal lacing of the *shikoro*. The samurai's pigtail of hair was allowed to pass through the *tehen*, the hole in the centre of the helmet's crown, where the plates met, either with or without a hat to cover it, which would give some extra protection. No armour was worn on the right arm so as to leave it free for drawing the bow, but a simple bag with sewn-on plates was worn on the left arm. This completed the costume of the samurai, with one overriding purpose in mind: to provide the maximum protection for a man who was a mounted archer. This role was so important that the samurai referred to their calling as *kyūba no michi*, or 'the way of horse and bow'.

The way of horse and bow

Kyūba no michi, like the later term *bushidō* 'the way of the warrior', (*michi* and *dō* are the same word), implies a certain élite status for these fine mounted archers which depended as much on their ancestry as on their martial prowess. A story in the twelfth-century *Konjaku Monogatari* contains the following grudging praise in its description of a warrior: 'Although he was not of a warrior house, he was brave and accomplished in the way of horse and bow.' The élite nature of the samurai is an important factor ro remember when considering the accounts of the period, because they were written for an aristocratic public who wished to read of the deeds of their own class, and preferably their own family's ancestors. The hundreds of footsoldiers who accompanied the samurai were almost totally ignored. For this reason the *gunkimono*, or 'war tales' have to be treated with some reservations as a historical record, and provide quite a contrast to the more sober accounts recorded in court diaries or official chronicles.

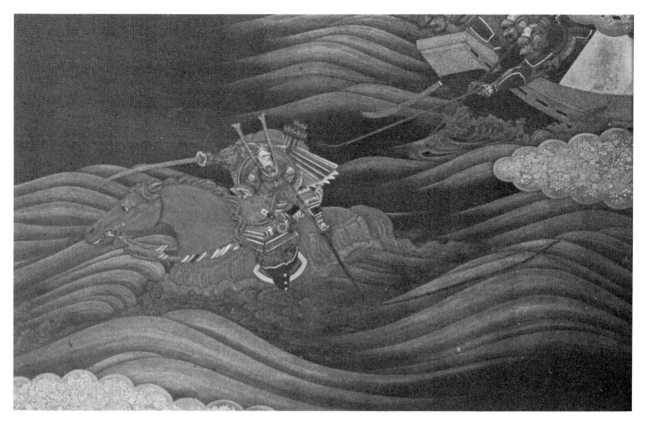

▲ The dropped bow It was important to a samurai that he maintain an image of a strong and skilled archer. The general Minamoto Yoshitsune was the nephew of the legendary Minamoto Tametomo, so when his own comparatively flimsy bow fell from his grasp during the battle of Yashima in 1184 he risked considerable personal injury in order to retrieve it. This incident is here illustrated on a lacquered tray. (Courtesy of Sotheby and Co.)

The *gunkimono* are invaluable, however, for the light they shed on samurai values and beliefs, and in particular the ideals which the samurai cherished as the exemplar for their behaviour in action. Much of the description is concerned with the samurai acting as an individual and aristocratic 'lone warrior', whose brave actions in single combat contribute to the overall victory. Similarly they can give very valuable information about the practice of the martial arts, for even if the incidents described were not actually performed by the character whose supposed exploits are being retold, the mode of combat and the use of various weaponry is described within a framework of a sound knowledge of the technical limitations of the arms and armour of the period, and there is a remarkable consistency between different *gunkimono* when it comes to describing single combat.

Several of the most important *gunkimono* have been translated fully or partially into English. The earliest of the genre, the *Shōmonki*, which deals with the rebellion of Taira Masakado, was written about the year AD 954 and contains little in the way of description of combat. The *Konjaku Monogatari*, which also includes Masakado among its wide-ranging subject matter, has several sections of great interest, some of which are used below. For the Gempei War period the *Hōgen Monogatari* and the *Heike Monogatari*, written in the mid thirteenth century, are the richest in their vivid details, as are certain parts of the later *Shōkyūki*, which deals with the rebellion of the ex-Emperor Go-Toba in 1221.

The archer in combat

At this time in Japanese history all combat, single or in the form of a pitched battle, began with the bow. There are references to mounted archers as early as AD 672, when the brother of the late Emperor Tenchi asserted his claim to the throne in a bold revolt against his usurping nephew, using the powerful striking force of a squad of mounted archers. Incidentally, it is in the description of this action that we also find the first use of the term *bugei* ('martial arts'). The design of the traditional Japanese bow which the samurai wielded is still that used today in the martial art of *kyūdo*. The bow was long, made from laminations of wood and bound with rattan. Owing to its

▼ **Archery Equipment** This page from the *Gunyōki* shows various gloves and other details required for archery.

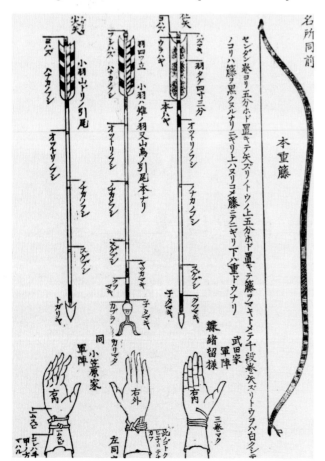

use from the saddle of a horse it was fired from about a third of the way up its length. A high level of accuracy resulted from hours of practice on ranges where the arrows were discharged at small wooden targets while the horse was galloping. This became the traditional art of *yabusame*, still performed at festivals, notably in the city of Kamakura. The archer, dressed nowadays in traditional hunting gear, discharges the bow at right angles to his direction of movement.

By the twelfth century there had been sufficient years of samurai warfare for successive generations to appreciate and value certain traditions and formalities of combat. There was an accepted ideal, for example, of a 'set-piece battle', which would begin by the firing of signal arrows high into the air over the enemy lines. Each arrow had a large, bulb-like perforated wooden head which whistled as it flew through the air. The sound was a call to the gods to draw their attention to the great deeds of bravery which were about to be performed by rival warriors. The samurai would then commence a fierce archery exchange, with varying degrees of success, and then one or more feats of individual combat. Such a contest would traditionally begin with one warrior calling out a challenge, in which he would recount at length his elaborate and honourable pedigree. The challenge would be answered from within the opposing army, thus providing a recognized mechanism whereby only worthy opponents would meet in combat.

One such encounter, in a form of a 'mock battle', is recorded in detail in *Konjaku Monogatari*. The occasion was that of a pre-arranged large-scale duel between two samurai rivals, who brought their war-bands together for a trial of strength. After a preliminary exchange of arrows they agreed that a better test of their skills would be individual combat. They drew up their horses some distance away from each other, and released their first arrows as they began to charge. The second arrows were fired in *yabusame* style as they passed at a gallop, and caused minor wounds. Each dodged the other's third arrow, fired from rest, after which they agreed that honour had been more than satisfied.

A bloody battle could be a very different matter. There was an archery duel and a series of challenges before the Battle of Kurikara in 1183, but for a very subtle purpose. Minamoto Yoshinaka planned to divide his forces and surround the Taira army, but how was he to cover these movements and hold the Taira in position? His solution

THE ARCHER IN COMBAT

was to conceal his manoeuvres by fighting a battle, but a battle so formal and so stylized that there would be no risk of his side being defeated, or any opportunity for the Taira to realize that the whole purpose was to confine them to this small area until night fell. Yoshinaka knew his history, and the demands of samurai tradition. The battle would begin with a duel of arrows, followed by individual combat. The proud Taira would give it their full concentration, hoping thereby to earn for themselves a name in the epic poetry that would be written about them in the future.

So the two armies faced each other in full battle array, at a distance of about 350 yards, but neither side advanced. After a while fifteen picked samurai from the Minamoto came forward between the armies, and each fired a signalling arrow at the Taira lines. Fifteen men of the Taira responded similarly. Then thirty Minamoto samurai advanced and fired arrows, against whom the Taira sent thirty more, and so on from fifty to a hundred. Then the hundred engaged one another in combat. These

activities continued throughout the day, and as the sun set Yoshinaka's decisive encircling force arrived at the rear in complete secrecy.

Most encounters, of course, did not allow such niceties of behaviour to take place, but the archery duel is often found, and the bow has an honourable place in the history of the samurai fighting arts. There are many examples of skill with the bow and arrow, notably the archer Minamoto Tametomo, who fought during the attack on the Shirakawa-den in the Hōgen Incident and shot many arrows clean through saddles, horses and his

▼ **An archery contest at the Sanjusangendō in Kyōto** One of the most ancient traditions associated with archery in Japan were the regular contests held at the Sanjusangendō, a temple in Kyōto. Arrows were fired the length of the front 'cloisters'. This much damaged woodblock illustration from the *Buke Chōkoki* shows one such contest taking place. (The smudges are the characters from the other side showing through the thin paper.)

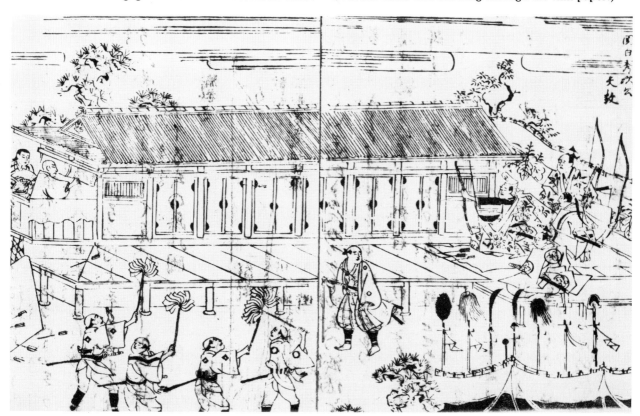

THE NOBLE SAMURAI

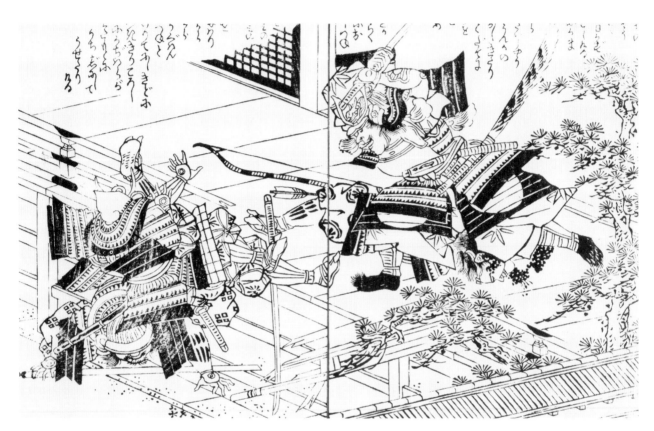

▲ Minamoto Yoshitsune One of the greatest individual warriors in the Gempei War was the general Minamoto Yoshitune. He here engages samurai of the Taira in hand-to-hand combat. (From the *Yoshitsune Ichidai-ki*)

opponents, as the *Hōgen Monogatari* tells us: 'The arrow pierced the breastplate of Ito Roku, who was first in the enemy's van, and passed through him, turned the sleeve of Ito Go's armour inside out and hung there. Ito Roku at once fell dead from his horse.' Later in the same action: 'Tametomo shot before him and his arrow whistled through the air. It pierced the pommel of Yamada's saddle, and cutting through the skirt of his armour and his own body too, went through the cantle and stuck out three inches beyond. For a moment he seemed to be held in the saddle by the arrow, but suddenly he fell head-first to the ground.' Minamoto Tametomo is also credited with using a bow and arrow to sink a ship belonging to the Taira! The massive arrowhead struck the overladen boat just above the waterline and split the planking. Nasu no

Yoichi is another famous name. At the Battle of Yashima in 1184 the Taira hung a fan from the mast of one of their ships and invited the Minamoto to shoot it down, hoping thereby to persuade them to waste precious arrows. Nasu no Yoichi hit the fan with his first arrow, even though he was on horseback in the water and the boat he was aiming at was bobbing up and down. Both these men represent the ideal to which all samurai aspired, that of the supreme warrior, whose individual skills shone forth even in the midst of battle, in the golden age of the noble samurai.

▶ Nasu no Yoichi hits the mark One of the most celebrated demonstrations of skill given by a mounted archer occurred at the Battle of Yashima in 1184. The Taira fastened a fan to the mast of one of their ships and challenged the Minamoto to bring it down. This drawing by Hokusai shows the young Nasu no Yoichi earning great glory for himself by hitting the fan with his first arrow, which greatly added to the morale of the Minamoto.

紙中限りあり
兵舩ハ運ふ
遠く箭ゑへ
軍くと打むし
軍し

那須の與市
宗高

扇に的の

2.

Close Combat during the Gempei War Period

The most glorious passages in the military romances of the *gunkimono* are concerned with the samurai performing his primary function: that of being a noble, individual mounted archer. The bow, like the Western gunslinger's Colt 45, allowed combat to take place at a distance, and on many occasions the issue of a challenge was settled by arrows fired from horseback. But once rivals closed, the nature of combat changed dramatically, and it is to this aspect of samurai behaviour that we now turn.

For close combat the bow would be handed to an attendant and cutting weapons were used, the best known of which, of course, was the famous 'samurai sword', which in those days was a *tachi*, a style of sword slung, cutting edge downwards, at the side of the armour from a strong belt. However, as was implied by the phrase *kyūba no michi*, a samurai's worth was measured in terms of his prowess with the bow, rather than the sword. Now to the modern mind the images of 'samurai' and 'sword' are almost inseparable. The sword has acquired a quasi-religious, almost mystical symbolism, and is wielded in a way that often appears to be a combination of superhuman skill and technological perfection. But in the Heian Period all the traditions to be associated with the Japanese sword lay in the future, including that of the lone, wandering samurai. More surprising perhaps, than the apparent absence of sword 'mystique', is the absence of sword 'technique', with a shortage of references to anything resembling swordplay, either from the saddle or on foot.

There is in fact only one incident in *Heike Monogatari* that implies sword combat while still mounted, when two comrades support each other as they lead an assault on the Taira fortress of Ichi-no-tani in 1184 (*Heike Monogatari*, vol. 9, chap. 10): '. . . Kumagai and Hirayama both bore themselves most valiantly, one charging forward when the other gave back, and neither yielding to the other in strength and boldness, hewing at the foe with loud shouts while the sparks flew from their weapons.' But this valiant charge (*see* illustration) is far from typical samurai behaviour. Time and again the actual pattern of combat seems to be the same. First, there is an archery contest between two mounted opponents. This may on occasions be resolved by a direct hit and a mortal wound, otherwise the two samurai immediately try to grapple with each other using the techniques later given the name *yoroi-gumi* ('armour

CLOSE COMBAT DURING THE GEMPEI WAR PERIOD

▲ **The exploits of Kumagai and Hirayama** The bold charge into the midst of the enemy by Kumagai Naozane and Hirayama Sueshige at the Battle of Ichi-no-tani in 1184 is the only mention in *Heike Monogatari* of swords being used from the saddle.

grappling'), also known as *kumi-uchi* or *katchū-gumi*. This would result in the unhorsing of one or both, at which point the *tantō* (dagger) is the weapon most favoured for close-quarter fighting. The sword is largely relegated to functioning as a device for providing the final *coup de grâce* by lopping off the head of an already vanquished enemy, or achieving the same end by a swift opportunistic stroke following the archery duel, as at the Battle of Shinohara (1183) in Sadler's translation of the *Heike Monogatari* (7, 6): 'Nyūzen, who was famous for the rapidity of his movements, catching him off guard, suddenly drew his sword and aimed a lightning thrust under his helmet.'

In the *Shōyūki*, which deals with ex-Emperor Go-Toba's rebellion of 1221, we read of a 'grapnel' (probably a polearm with several hooks at the end) allowing a sword to be used in a similar way (in McCullough's translation): '. . . he rushed up and hooked his grapnel into the crown of Satsuma's helmet, pulled him close, and struck off his head'. Several examples of similar practice are recorded in *Heike Monogatari*. But, as noted above, the other important edged weapon which the samurai kept about his person was the *tantō*, or dagger, and in fact the impression one gets in reading contemporary accounts of individual combat is that this *tantō* was much more important than the sword in deciding the outcome of a one-to-one *yoroi-gumi* contest. There are many examples of *tantō* use in combat. Take Sadler's translation of the account of a fight that eventually led to the death of Taira Tadanori in *Heike Monogatari* (9, 14):

'But Satsuma-no-kami, who had been brought up at Kumano, was famous for his strength, and was extremely active and agile besides, so clutching Tadazumi he pulled him from his horse, dealing him two stabs with his dirk while he was yet in the saddle, and following them with another as he was falling. The first two blows fell on his armour and failed to pierce it, while the third wounded him in the face but was not mortal . . .'

Or, at the same battle, (Ichi-no-tani, 1184), the single combat between Etchū Zenji Moritoshi and Inomata Noritsuna, which began with unarmed techniques, (*Heike Monogatari*, 9, 13):

'Rushing upon each other, they grappled fiercely so that both fell from their horses . . . he gripped his adversary and pinned him down so that he could not rise. Thus prostrate beneath his foe, try how he would to shift him or draw his sword, he could not so much as stir a finger to the hilt, and even when he strove to speak, so great was the pressure that no word would come forth.'

The intervention of a third party allows a pause in the combat, but soon they return to the fray:

'. . . he suddenly sprang up from the ground and dealt Moritoshi a heavy blow on the breastplate with his closed fist. Losing his balance at this unexpected

CLOSE COMBAT DURING THE GEMPEI WAR PERIOD

attack, Moritoshi fell over backwards, when Inomata immediately leapt upon him, snatched his dagger from his side, and pulling up the skirt of his armour, stabbed him so deeply thrice that the hilt and fist went in after the blade. Having thus dispatched him he cut off his head . . .'

In the *Shōkyūki* we have a full account of an archery duel concluded by a *yoroi-gumi* fight using *tantō*:

'Pulling an outer arrow from his quiver and fitting it to his rattan-striped bow, he drew the shaft to its full length and let fly. The arrow pierced the breastplate of Takeda Rokurō's chief retainer, who was standing at the left side of his lord, and shot through to the clover-leaf bow (the *agemaki*) at the armour's back,

◄ **The single combat between Etchū Zenji Moritoshi and Inomata Noritsuna** The *Heike Monogatari* contains this classic account of *yoroi-gumi* (see accompanying text).

◀ **The use of grapnels** By means of a hooked grapnel a samurai could be pulled from his horse and killed by sword and dagger. This illustration from the *Ehon Taikō-ki* is of a much later date than the Gempei Wars, but shows clearly of what these crude weapons consisted, and how they were used.

toppling the retainer instantly from his horse. Saburō shot again, and his second arrow passed completely through the neck bone of one of Takeda Rokurō's pages. Then Rokurō and Saburō grappled together and fell from their horses. As they tumbled back and forth, Saburō drew his dagger and pulled the crown of Rokurō's helmet down as far as the shoulder straps of his armour. Rokurō looked to be in danger, but just at that moment Takeda Hachirō came upon the scene, and pushing Rokurō aside, cut off his assailant's head.'

All this evidence, of course, stands in direct contrast to the usually accepted theory that the Japanese sword developed as a fairly long, curved-bladed weapon so that it could more easily be wielded from the saddle. One may perhaps hypothesize that the reason for the *yoroi-gumi* style of combat was largely determined by the samurai's primary role as a mounted archer. While mounted and wearing a suit of armour built like a rigid box, he was effectively a mobile 'gun platform'. When unable to wield his bow he was ungainly and unwieldy, able only to grapple in the most clumsy fashion while wearing a defensive costume that, although not unduly heavy, was not designed to allow him to take the fight to the enemy, and was certainly not helpful in allowing a sword to be used from the saddle in the way for which it was intended. Kammer, in his introduction to his translation of the *Tengu Geijutsu-ron*, in fact suggests that the essential reason for the dominance of the bow over the sword, at least during the earlier period, was simply one of expense, putting good swords in short supply. We do know that the number of swordsmiths almost quadrupled during the century following the Gempei War, which may in part account for the greater use of the sword in that latter period.

The sword duel

Even when on foot the box-like design of the *yoroi* continued to hamper the movements of all but the

▲ **A samurai with a *tantō*** The *tantō*, or dagger, was the most frequently used edged weapon in the *yoroi-gumi* grappling combats of the Gempei War. (Ivory statuette — photograph courtesy of Christie's)

strongest samurai. Circumstantial evidence for this is provided by that fact that one of the few accounts of 'sword-fighting' in the pages of *Heike Monogatari*, and certainly one of the liveliest, is demonstrated not by one of these élite mounted samurai, but by a more lightly clad monk who probably had little in the way of body armour beyond a simple *dō-maru*, a corselet that was wrapped round the torso. The monk, Tsutsui Jomyō Meishū, was a *sohei*, or warrior priest, of the temple of Mii-dera. The occasion was the First Battle of Uji in 1180. The retreating Minamoto army, accompanied by their monk allies, had torn up the planking on the bridge at Uji to delay pursuit by the Taira, and had taken their stand on the far bank of the river. One group of mounted Taira

▲ **The fight on the bridge** An unusual illustration of the single combat across the broken bridge of Uji, this time from the *Gempei Seisuki*. The illustration covers two successive openings of the book.

---

samurai charged out of the morning mist and went straight through the hole on the bridge, but then the fight developed into a series of arrow duels, and individual combat across the broken beams. Having wielded bow and *naginata* (the form of glaive which was the monk's traditional weapon) Jomyō drew his sword, and:

> '. . . wielding it in the zig-zag style, the interlacing, cross, reverse dragonfly, waterwheel and eight sides at once styles of fencing, and cutting down eight men; but as he brought down the ninth with an exceeding mighty blow on the helmet the blade snapped at the hilt and fell splash into the water beneath. Then seizing the dirk which was his only weapon left he plied it as one in the death fury.'

This fascinating account (*Heike Monogatari* 4, 12) also confirms the existence, by the mid thirteenth century at least, of several styles of *kenjutsu*, and it is certain that

samurai were taught swordfighting techniques. It is not clear, however, how far such techniques were disseminated, whether 'schools' were established, or, for that matter, what was actually taught. The legends of the great hero Minamoto Yoshitsune credit his swordsmanship skills to the tutorship of the goblins, half man and half crow, called *tengu*, who inhabited the forests of Mount Kurama, and whose swordfighting skills were said to be superb. The young hero, dodging the blows of the *tengu* among the trees, has long been a popular subject for Japanese artists.

Yet whatever training a samurai may have received, the nature of his primary role made it impossible for such skills to be used much in battle, so that in the majority of cases the 'sword stage', implied by the succession of bow, *naginata*, sword and *tantō* in the Jomyō story, was

---

▶ **The monk Jomyō at the Battle of Uji** One of the most celebrated feats of swordsmanship in *Heike-Monogatari* is performed not by a samurai but by a warrior monk called Tsutsui Jomyō Meishū. In this book illustration by Hokusai Jomyō vaults over his comrade Tajima to enter the fray.

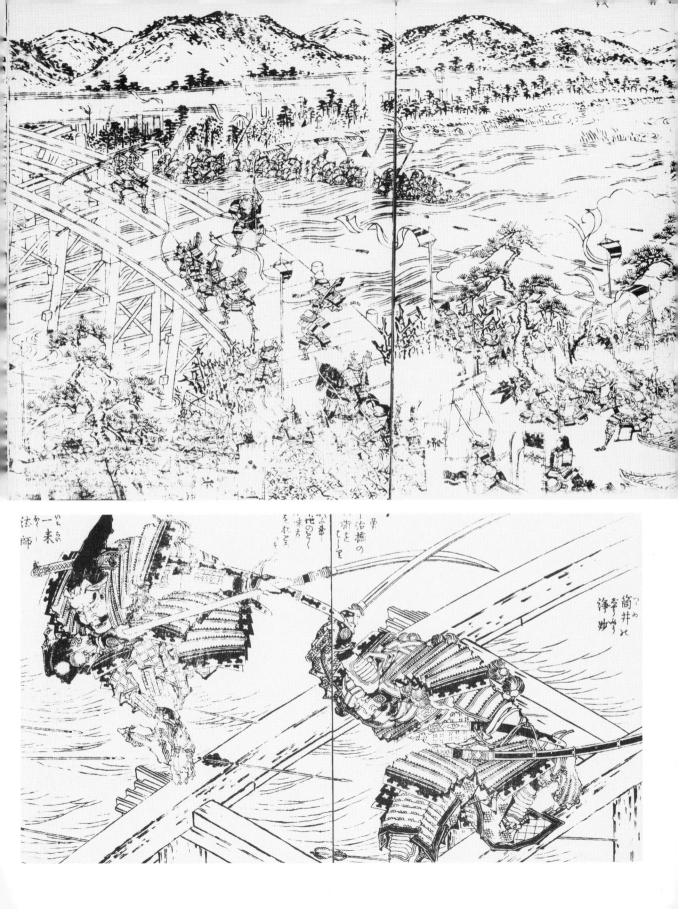

◄ **The swordfight of Kajiwara Genda** When not mounted on his horse the samurai could wield his sword more freely, though he was still encumbered somewhat by the design of the *yoroi* armour. In this illustration to *Heike Monogatari* (vol. 9, chap 11) we see Kajiwara Genda '. . . dismounted and fighting on foot, for his horse had been shot from under him, with his helmet struck off from his head and his long hair flying in the wind, his back against a rock twenty feet high, and two of his retainers on his left and right fighting desperately with five soldiers of the Heike'.

---

simply missed out. However, if there were time to dismount successfully from a fallen horse some excellent swordplay could be seen, displayed by samurai whose desire to survive overcame any disadvantages posed by their armour, as at the Battle of Shinohara (*Heike Monogatari* 7, 6):

> 'Arikuni, having penetrated very deeply into the ranks of the foe, had his horse shot from under him, and then while he was fighting on foot, his helmet was struck from his head, so that he looked like a youth fighting, with his long hair streaming in all directions. By this time his arrows were exhausted, so he drew his sword and laid about him mightily, until, pierced by seven or eight shafts, he met his death still on his feet and glaring at his enemies.'

There is a similar description of Kajiwara Genda's desperate fight at Ichi-no-tani (*see* illustration). During the fight at Mizushima (1183), fought on board ship and thus unencumbered by horses, we also see some swordplay (*Heike Monogatari* 8, 8): 'And so shouting their warcry, they began the fight, drawing their bows and pouring in a hail of arrows until they came to close quarters, when they drew their swords and engaged one another hand to hand.'

In spite of such accounts there is ample evidence that skill with a bow was the most prized accomplishment, and this feeling was not confined to the battlefield. There is a very telling anecdote in *Konjaku Monogatari*. One night a certain Norimitsu was attacked by robbers while on his way to visit a female acquaintance. He was armed only with a sword: 'Norimitsu crouched down and looked around, but as he could not see any sign of a bow, but only a great glittering sword, he thought with relief, "It's not a bow at any rate."' He did in fact vanquish the robbers, but his evident relief that he was not up against bowmen is in complete contrast to the later image of the samurai swordsman. Similar sentiments are expressed by the warrior Mionoya Jurō at the Battle of Yashima in 1184, who makes a different, but equally unexpected comparison in *Heike Monogatari* (11, 6): 'When he saw the warrior behind the shield come to meet him flourishing a huge *naginata* he knew that his own small sword would be useless, and blew on a conch and retreated.' The very next incident described in the narrative puts the final seal on the importance of the image of a samurai as a skilled archer. The Minamoto commander, Yoshitsune, accidentally drops his bow into the sea, and puts himself at some personal risk in his effort to retrieve it. When his older retainers reproach him he replies, 'It was not that I grudged the bow . . . and if the bow were one that required two or three men to bend it, like that of my uncle Tametomo, they would be quite welcome to it, but I should not like a weak one like mine to fall into the hands of the enemy for them to laugh at it . . .'

The naginata

There are few accounts in the *Heike Monogatari* of samurai wielding the other edged weapon mentioned above, the *naginata*, which was looked on as a weapon for the common footsoldier, or for the warrior monks. Tajima, a comrade of the monk Tsutsui Jōmyō Meishū, the hero of Uji, used his *naginata* to good effect in his own combat on the broken bridge (*Heike Monogatari* 4, 12):

> 'Then Gochin-no-Tajima, throwing away the sheath of his long *naginata*, strode forth alone on to the bridge, whereupon the Heike straightaway shot at him fast and furious. Tajima, not at all perturbed, ducking to avoid the higher ones and leaping up over those that flew low, cut through those that flew straight with his whirring *naginata*, so that even the enemy looked on in admiration. Thus it was that he was dubbed "Tajima the arrow-cutter".'

The *naginata* eventually came to be regarded as a weapon suitable also for women, and woodblock prints of the Edo Period frequently show a *naginata* being wielded by Tomoe Gozen, the wife of Minamoto Yoshinaka. In the *Heike Monogatari* (9, 4), however, when she

CLOSE COMBAT DURING THE GEMPEI WAR PERIOD

and her husband are defeated and surrounded, she has no *naginata*, but plunges into the midst of the enemy to grapple with a worthy opponent, and '. . . flung herself upon Onda and grappling with him dragged him from his horse, pressed him calmly against the pommel of her saddle, and cut off his head', with, one presumes, either a sword or a *tantō*.

Thus by the middle of the thirteenth century the notion was well-established that the ideal of the samurai warrior was that of the brave, élite individual, essentially fighting alone, even in the middle of a huge battle, skilled most of all in mounted archery and to whom swordplay was a valued art that was unfortunately allowed little rein. It was to take a major shock to change these ideas, and provide any alternative mode of combat. This shock came from China in 1274.

▶ **Tajima the arrow-cutter** An ivory statuette from Manchester Museum depicting the other monk hero of the First Battle of Uji, 'Tajima the arrow-cutter', who whirled his *naginata* to deflect arrows fired at him by the Taira archers.

▼ **Tomoe Gozen takes a head** In this detail from an illustration in *Heike Monogatari* Tomoe Gozen pulls an enemy from his saddle and cuts his head off using her *tantō*.

3.

Challenge to the Samurai

The prize which the samurai won by means of their 'way of horse and bow' was the establishment of a military government in the form of the *bakufu*, or Shogunate. But the Minamoto family, whose personal supremacy seemed as well assured as that of the *bakufu* itself, did not have long to enjoy their power, for within three generations they were supplanted by the Hōjō, who ruled Japan until 1333.

The first challenge to the Hōjō came not from a rival samurai family, but from a retired emperor who in 1221 tried to overthrow the *bakufu* and re-establish the imperial power. The accounts in the *Shōkyūki*, quoted in the previous chapter, which refer to ex-Emperor Go-Toba's abortive attempt to restore the old imperial power, give the impression of a style of samurai warfare essentially unchanged from the heroic days of the Gempei War. There are archery combats, challenges to worthy opponents, and all the tradition of the élite lone warrior that was now so engrained into the samurai psyche. Not that there was any pressure for this to change. There were no technological developments in arms and armour, and little in the way of rebellions. In fact there is some evidence that fighting skills declined during the times of peace.

The Mongol invasions

The great challenge came fifty years later, when, not for the last time in Japanese history, the impetus to question the nature of samurai warfare came from abroad. This time it came in the shape of the first attempt by the Mongol Emperor Kublai Khan to invade Japan in 1274.

The circumstances surrounding both wars against the Mongol invaders (they returned in 1281) have been obscured by the famous '*coup de grâce*' delivered on both occasions by the weather, the storm of 1281 being so sudden and so fierce that it was immediately dubbed the *kami-kaze*, or 'Divine Tempest', sent by the Sun-Goddess to aid her people. (It was this term, *kami-kaze*, that the suicide pilots of the Second World War adopted as their title, thus identifying themselves with the successful destruction of an invader.) Decisive though the typhoon was, it would have been minimal in its effectiveness if the determination and fighting qualities of the samurai had not forced the entire fleet to lie at anchor with all their armies on board, unable to establish a beachhead because of the tenacity with which the land was defended. In fact, the samurai, although outnumbered, not

熊谷直実

THE MONGOL INVASIONS

◄ **The mounted samurai** A modern statue at Suma, showing the style of armour that was worn up to the time of the Mongol Invasions.

only held their ground but took the battle to the Mongol ships. They seized the military initiative by a series of raids in little boats, led by daring warriors who vied with one another to capture the highest ranking enemies in a kind of daredevil game. One of these epics is recorded in a famous narrative picture scroll which a certain samurai had painted to support his claim for reward.

If the Mongol invasions taught the samurai anything to do with the fighting arts it was surely that intelligence is a martial virtue. The tradition in which these young warriors were steeped was one of individual honour and prowess, supported by precedent and myth going back two centuries. The notions of individual combat and the giving and receiving of challenges were their stock-in-trade, yet suddenly they were faced with an alien enemy, with no common language in which challenges could be delivered, and a foreign tradition of non-élite footsoldier archers who shot arrows by the hundred in massed volleys. That was the overall lesson of the Mongol

invasions. But what was actually learned in military terms? Did it cause anything beyond a temporary re-think of tactics?

The first experience was on the island of Tsushima, which lies between Japan and Korea. In the lively words of Yamada's account, they:

'. . . advanced in phalanx, which was also a novelty to the Japanese, protecting themselves most effectually with their shields . . . The Mongolian shafts harassed them terribly; still all the Japanese soldiers fought according to their own etiquette of battle. A humming arrow, the sign of commencing the combat, was shot. The Mongols greeted it with a shout of derision. Then some of the best fighters among the Japanese advanced in their usual dignified, leisurely manner and formulated their traditional challenge. But the Mongol phalanx, instead of sending out a single warrior to answer the defiance,

▼ **A duel with swords** This picture from the *Ehon Taikō-ki* depicts a serious duel with real swords. If a fight were staged merely to establish the superiority of a school, or of a technique, wooden *bokutō* would be substituted.

CHALLENGE TO THE SAMURAI

opened their ranks, enclosed each challenger, and cut him to pieces. The invaders moved in unchanging formation, obeying signals from their commanding officers.'

The futility of attempting individual combat was brought home to a samurai called Sukesada (his surname is unknown) who killed twenty-four Mongols in hand-to-hand swordfighting on the army's flank, where a grove of trees conveniently broke up the Mongol phalanx. As Sukesada became progressively isolated his challenges became the louder, but were eventually ended not with a further worthy opponent, but with a shower of arrows, three of which pierced his chest.

Contemporary accounts show that in spite of these shock encounters on the beaches, the samurai clung stubbornly to being mounted archers, only dismounting from their horses when necessary to engage the swarms of Mongol, Chinese and Korean warriors in bitter hand-to-hand combats. Yet somehow the samurai spirit asserted itself in its manifestation as the brave lone warrior. We noted above the 'hit and run' raids on the Mongol fleet, often successfully terminated by bringing home a pile of severed heads, and some individual archery combats occurred on land in a manner every bit as glorious as the deeds of their ancestors. One such example is the archery of three generations of the Shōni family, who demonstrated to their enemies that the Japanese style of individual marksmanship with a bow could be every bit as effective as random volley firing. Shōni Kakuie was the governor of Dazaifu. During the second invasion of 1281 he was in charge of a combined operation which aimed to push the Mongol fleet further out into the bay by seaborne attack, while a mounted army speedily reinforced the coastal area where a detachment of the Mongol army was expected to attempt its next landing. He was accompanied on the land-based half of the operation by his son Kagesuke, and his twelve-year-old grandson Suketoki, who, the story tells us, threatened to commit suicide if he were not allowed to ride with the army, and was only prevented from ending his life by his grandfather's catching hold of his arm as the blade of his *tantō* was about to pierce his skin.

The arrival of the Shōni force put great heart into the defenders, who rallied to the attack, but there was a grave danger of the Japanese army being surrounded by a vastly outnumbering Mongol force, who poured their

▶ **Mounted archery In this section from the *Ehon Taikō-ki* a samurai demonstrates his skill in firing a bow from horseback, the primary accomplishment expected from a samurai. The incident depicted is of the sixteenth century, but the techniques are identical with those used during the times of the Mongol invasions.**

customary showers of arrows down upon them. At this point the grandson Suketoki, with supreme confidence, rode up to the Mongol lines where he had spotted a person who was obviously of very senior rank. Ignoring the fact that the Mongols could not speak Japanese Shōni Suketoki announced his name and intentions, put an arrow to his bow, and, without waiting for a reply, shot the Mongol general clean through the chest.

It turned out to be just the opportunity the Japanese had been looking for, and proud grandfather Shōni Kakuie led the samurai in a charge into the midst of the Mongols, whereupon fierce hand-to-hand fighting took place. The battle continued until nearly dark, when Kakuie withdrew his troops to the safety of the Japanese fortified lines. One by one the stragglers withdrew, until only the contingent commanded by Kakuie's son Kagesuke was left, and they were being pursued vigorously by a number of Mongol horsemen led by another general. As they came within bowshot Shōni Kagesuke suddenly turned in his saddle and put a well-aimed arrow into the Mongol leader. It turned out later that his victim was one of the three chief commanders of the entire Mongol invasion force, a man known to the Japanese as Ryū Fukukō.

The archetypal single combat of the Mongol invasions remains, however, the 'little ship' raids by the Japanese on the Mongol fleet, particularly during the 1281 expedition. The most famous of these was led by a certain Kōno Michiari, who set out in broad daylight with two boatloads of samurai. Thinking they had come to offer surrender terms the Mongols let them come alongside, at which the Japanese sprang on to the ship. Kōno Michiari killed the captain and escaped under cover of the burning vessel, taking another high ranking officer as captive.

The experience of defeating the Mongols was one never to be forgotten, and the exploits of the warriors joined

▶ **A samurai stabs using his *wakizashi* The *wakizashi* was the shorter of the pair of swords traditionally carried by samurai.**

THE WAR BETWEEN THE COURTS

つちやそうざう
土屋惣蔵
いきせ
憤馳せ
あやべだいかうすけ
蹄部大炊助
を射後す

those of their ancestors in the amalgam of myth and tradition that was to carry them through another six centuries. It is unlikely, however, that there were many changes in the martial arts as a direct result of the experience, apart from a realization that appropriate styles of combat and behaviour could change with circumstances. The style of armour changed not at all, indicating that the role of the mounted archer had emerged largely unscathed. Perhaps one discovery was the confirmation that the Japanese sword was vastly superior to its continental counterparts, and could be much better used than it had been.

The war between the courts

The realization that styles of fighting should change when circumstances required was reinforced sixty years later when Japan was once again split by civil war. These wars, the Nambokuchō Wars, the 'Wars between the Northern and Southern Courts', arose from an attempt by the

Emperor Go-Daigo to overthrow the Shogunate in 1333. It was an anachronistic gesture almost doomed to fail before it had begun, and its long-term result was merely the substitution of one dynasty of Shoguns by another, and a long and bitterly fought civil war that lasted sporadically for sixty years.

Our major source for the study of samurai warfare during the Nambokuchō Wars is the *Taiheiki*, a work which ranks with the *Heike Monogatari* in the vivid picture it paints of the fighting arts of the time. It was composed in about the mid fourteenth century, a century later than *Heike Monogatari*, and is probably much more reliable as a historical document. But what does it tell us about the martial arts in the fourteenth century? Is there evidence of a major change since the Gempei War? Once again, the answer would seem to be 'no'. The early chapters in the *Taiheiki* bear a remarkable resemblance to the *Heike Monogatari* in their descriptions of samurai warfare. There is a vivid account of a single combat between a monk armed with a *naginata* and a mounted samurai (my translation):

'Just then a monk kicked over the shield in front of him and sprang forward, whirling his *naginata* like a waterwheel. It was Kajitsu of Harima. Kaitō received him with his right arm, meaning to cut down into his helmet bowl, but the glancing sword struck down lightly from Kajitsu's shoulder plate to the cross stiching at the bottom of his armour. Again Kaitō struck forcefully, but his left foot broke through its stirrup, and he was likely to fall from his horse. As he straightened his body, Kajitsu thrust up his *naginata*, and two or three times drove its point quickly into his helmet. Kaitō fell off his horse, pierced cleanly through the throat.'

Subsequent operations, however, required a reassessment every bit as urgent as the threat posed by the Mongol invasions, because the Nambokuchō Wars developed into a long process of defending fortified camps in wooded mountainous districts. The samurai who supported the Emperor Go-Daigo and his descendants, who maintained his legitimacy even after the Ashikaga clan had become Shoguns and set up another Emperor in Kyōto, thus fought what was largely a guerrilla war in the forests and mountains of central Japan, either to defend Go-Daigo's person, or to harass various armies and draw them away from him.

▶ **Benkei in action** The fiercest *naginata* fighter of all was the giant Benkei, the companion of Yoshitsune. Here he wields his *naginata* to good effect against enemy samurai in an illustration from the *Yoshitsune Ichidai-ki*. Similar fighting techniques were used long into the fourteenth century.

This style of warfare became almost inevitable because of the great imbalance in forces between the two sides, and the process began almost as soon as Go-Daigo announced his intentions of overthrowing the *bakufu*. Remembering the fate of the previous century's rebellion by Go-Toba, which had collapsed quickly when faced with a rapid military response from Kamakura, Go-Daigo and his followers fled from Kyōto, taking with them the crown jewels, and entrenched themselves on Mount Kasagi. Thus the trend of the war developed, the *bakufu* forces attacking a series of fortified 'castles' on Mount Hiei and Kasagi, then the progressively stronger foundations of Akasaka and Chihaya, commanded by the great commander Kusunoki Masashige: '. . . the warriors within the castle threw down mighty rocks from the tower tops to smash the enemy's shields; and while the attackers were afflicted the defenders shot at them fiercely with arrows'. These are tactics not unlike the defence of the Shirakawa-den in *Hōgen Monogatari*, where wooden walls protected samurai against a fierce exchange of arrows. But there are certain important differences. First, it was on terrain over which mounted fighting was largely impracticable, so the horse became just a means of approaching the scene of battle, and second, the nature of the ground allowed the use of rocks, pits and booby traps as a weapon. I visited both Akasaka and Chihaya in 1986, and can confirm the difficulty of the terrain. Take away the modern roads and the problems facing an attacker fall into perspective. The forests are dense, and the fall of the ground quite precipitous in places. Chihaya is particularly dramatic, and must have been a death trap to an army unfamiliar with the layout of these wild forested hills.

On one occasion Kusunoki allowed the *bakufu* army to approach on horseback along the forest paths until they were quite close to the fortified line, then felled five great trees on top of them, and poured arrows down into the confused scene. On another occasion: '. . . when the wall was about to fall, those within the castle took ladles with

THE WAR BETWEEN THE COURTS

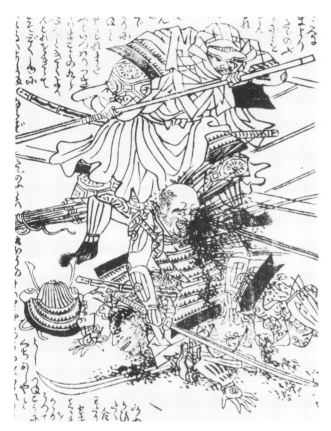

▲ **The site of Chihaya castle** The castle, scene of Kusunoki Masashige's desperate defence against the *bakufu* army, was constructed around the peaks and crags of the heavily wooded Chihayayama, shown here as it appears today.

▼ **Dropping rocks** A model at the Minatogawa Shrine Museum showing the defence of a castle by dropping rocks on to the attackers. This was a technique used by Kusunoki Masashige.

handles ten or twenty feet long, collected boiling water, and poured it on to them. The hot water passed through the holes in their helmet tops, ran down from the edges of their shoulder guards, and burned their bodies so severely that they fled in terror, throwing down their shields and grapnels.'

One of the most dramatic scenarios of all was Kusunoki Masashige's response to a plan by the *bakufu* forces that looked every bit as clever as his own schemes for defence. They had built a prefabricated bridge, dropped across a chasm by some form of pulley mechanism:

'But Kusunoki's men threw lighted torches on to the bridge, piling them up like stacks of firewood . . . and with a pump pumped out oil like a flowing waterfall. As the beams of the bridge took fire, the wind from

the valley below fanned and spread the flames . . . yet behind them pressed on the mighty host, heedless of trouble ahead . . . until the beams burned through and the bridge fell down abruptly to the bottom of the chasm. Even so must be the torment of sinners in the eight great Buddhist hells, transfixed on sword trees and sword mountains, or burned by fierce fires and vats of molten iron!'

With such intense fighting going on throughout the country for six decades, it is unsurprising that it had an effect on the martial arts. The most noticeable change

▼ **Guarding the parapet at Chihaya A model at the Minatogawa Shrine museum showing the crude wooden parapets that made up the defences of Kusunoki Masashige's fortresses.**

THE WAR BETWEEN THE COURTS

was in the samurai's costume. The evidence presented by extant specimens of armour from this time indicates that the bulky, box-like suit of armour known as *yoroi* was gradually phased out in favour of a lighter, more 'streamlined' design based on the *dō-maru* (wrap round) style worn by the footsoldiers, which, like the *yoroi*, was suspended from the shoulders, but fastened tightly round the body. To the casual glance there seems very little difference between the two, but the new styles based on the *dō-maru* acknowledged the need for an armour to provide more than a passive defence for a mounted archer. As the heavy and wide skirt pieces of the *yoroi* were replaced by several smaller *kusazuri* (a style of armour-making that was to last for the rest of samurai history), the lack of solidity was compensated by introducing the *haidate*, a form of thigh guard rather like an

armoured apron, which was worn under the *dō*. A final response to fighting on foot was the substitution of *waraji* (simple, disposable straw sandals) for the elaborate fur boots of the mounted warrior. The most important developments, however, came not in the field of armour but of weapons, and in particular the use of the sword, as the samurai changed from being a mounted archer to a dismounted swordsman. This is the real beginning of the image, and the cult, of the lone warrior, and is the topic we will explore in the chapter which follows.

▼ **A *no-dachi* An innovation of the fourteenth century was the introduction of the *no-dachi*, an extra-long sword that was halfway between a sword and a polearm. This book illustration by Hokusai shows how the *no-dachi* was customarily worn slung across the back.**

4.

The Triumph of the Sword

We saw in the previous chapter how increasing opportunities to fight dismounted allowed the further development of close combat techniques, particularly those involving the sword. The written accounts of the period do indicate that the bow was still very important, but from the mid fourteenth century onwards the sword really comes into its own. There was no need to grab for a *tantō* as two horsemen clashed. Instead a preponderance of fighting on foot meant that swords could be used as freely as they had been intended. It is probably for this reason that we see a change in the design of the *shikoro*, the helmet neckguard, which was raked back and lifted up higher to enable the warrior to wield his weapon with more ease.

The samurai sword

The increase in warlike activity at these times was accompanied by a peak of achievement in the manufacture of the weapons the samurai were to employ, notably in the field of swordmaking. The Japanese sword is an extraordinary object, and the most remarkable thing about it is that it exists at all. Compare any museum's rusty specimens of medieval European knights' swords with their gleaming Japanese contemporaries, and it is easy to see how the very weapon itself acquired a legendary life of its own. Even its making is shrouded in mystery, because none of the great swordsmiths ever wrote down one of their secrets for its manufacture. Everything was passed on from master to favoured pupil, based entirely on practical experience gained over centuries, and without the guidance of any metallurgical or other scientific principles.

The making of a Japanese sword consisted of a series of complex activities. First of all came the production of a workable quantity of steel from iron ore, which was then worked into a composite blade. There was a hardening process, and a final shaping and polishing.

The first stage was a very laborious one, at the end of which the swordsmith possessed the bar of tool steel which could be then subjected to a remarkable, but well-authenticated process of hammering, notching and folding. By this method the single plate was beaten out, then deeply notched, folded over, and again hot-forged so that the surfaces welded tightly together. This process was repeated sometimes as many as thirty times, producing

THE SAMURAI SWORD

◄ **A fight to the death** Two samurai fight to the death in front of the Shogun. (Lone Wolf and Cub © 1989 First Publishing Inc. and Global Communications Corp.)

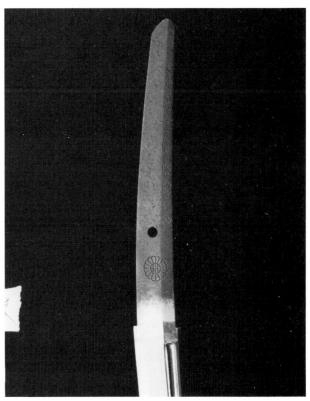

▲▼ **The *tachi*** The *tachi* is the form of Japanese sword that is carried slung from a belt with the cutting edge downwards. There is an inscription on the *nakago*, or tang. (Courtesy of Sotheby and Co.)

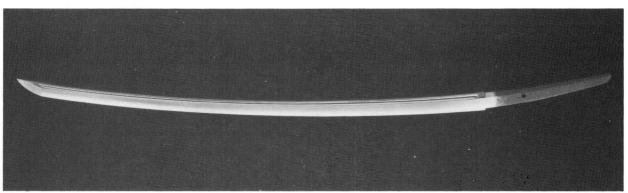

THE TRIUMPH OF THE SWORD

numerous laminations in the steel structure. Mathematics shows that the resulting number of layers produced by such a process will be 2 to the power of 'n', where n is the number of times it is repeated, so in a bar folded thirty times this would result in 10,736,461,824 layers! Even twenty repeat foldings would produce a million tiny sword-blades welded to one another, giving the blade a tremendous strength, and the capacity to be ground to a very sharp edge.

No smith, however, was satisfied to produce a sword from just one piece of tool steel. For all but the simplest daggers, the blade was of composite construction to make a sword that combined an extreme hardness, and therefore potential sharpness, in its cutting edge, with a resilient cushion for a body. To achieve this an envelope of quench-hardened tool steel was wrapped around a core of soft, low-carbon laminated steel. A few sword-smiths used an even more complicated arrangement of three or four types of steel bound together.

The crude swordblade was then shaped until it was almost at its final form, leaving very little metal to be removed in sharpening and polishing. It was then prepared for heating and selective quench-hardening, which involved plunging the hot blade into cool water. To make sure that the back of the blade, which would take the shock waves of a cut, was not itself hardened, the whole blade was encased in a stiff paste of clay and water, which was scraped away almost completely from the cutting edge. The blade was then brought to the desired temperature (monitored solely by colour, and one of the crucial 'trade secrets'), then placed horizontally into a trough of water, again kept at a critical and secret temperature. One of the many legends about the old swordsmiths tells of a greedy apprentice who attempted to discover the secret of the correct tempera-ture of the trough by putting his fingers into it, and was swiftly punished by having his hand instantly cut off by· a swordstroke from the furious master. The resulting blade then received its final shaping and polishing to bring out its full and terrible beauty, of which the most noticeable feature was the wavy line that indicated where the super-hard cutting edge met the body of the sword, its edge pattern following the boundary of the insulating clay.

This was the method that served the swordsmiths well throughout the centuries of their craft. Of swordsmiths known to us by name, the numbers had grown from about 450 in the Heian Period to 1,550 in the Kamakura Period. As the fourteenth century gave way to the fifteenth the numbers jumped to about 3,550. Many of the greatest names were active at this time, and of the outstanding craftsmen none was more celebrated than Masamune, who was alive at about the time of the Mongol invasions.

The mounted archers of the Gempei War had used a *tachi* style of sword, which was carried with the cutting edge downwards, but with most fighting now being carried out dismounted the *tachi* type of sword was felt to be a disadvantage owing to its length, and was gradually replaced by the somewhat shorter *katana*. Simultaneous with this development was the abandon-ment of the slung scabbard, which had required the use of two hands to draw the sword. Instead a trend developed towards a scabbard thrust through the belt, the sword's cutting edge being uppermost. From such an arrangement the sword could be withdrawn by a single controlled whiplash movement which would result in the fatal blow. This was the technique of *i-ai*, 'drawing the sword'. It was still difficult to perform when armoured, however, and many illustrations still depict a sword slung from a belt on the battlefield, but thrust through the belt in 'civilian dress'.

Perhaps because of tales taken home by the survivors of the Mongol invasions, or more likely because of the destructive effects of Japanese pirates, the inhabitants of continental Asia had by the beginning of the fifteenth century acquired a healthy respect for the qualities of the Japanese sword. Thus when, under the influence of the Shogun Ashikaga Yoshimitsu (who initiated the building of the famous 'Golden Pavilion'), Japan began to trade with Ming China, swords were among the objects most in demand. Initially they were needed for use against the pirates, but as Yoshimitsu took pains to demonstrate his determination to curtail this aspect of his countrymen's activity by boiling a few of them alive, this need disappeared. The largest quantity shipped over in one consignment actually totalled 30,000, which led to a major disagreement over the price. It would appear that the present-day concern over Japanese exports is nothing new! What is interesting from the point of view of samurai fighting arts is the fact that the Japanese sword is commonly regarded as a very precious and symbolic individual weapon, yet here we have evidence of mass production.

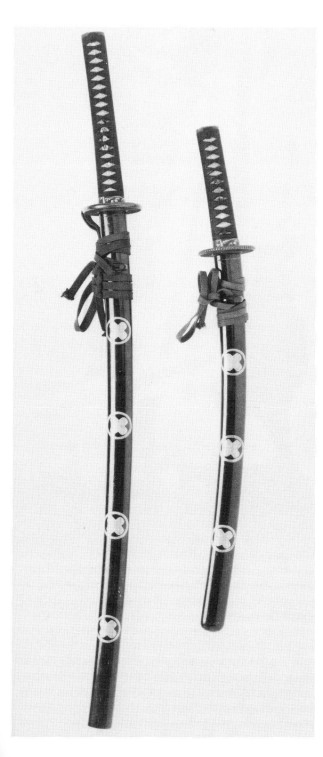

The early schools

Coincident with the growth in sword production, we see for the first time the emergence of a number of authenticated, rather than merely legendary, specialists in teaching swordsmanship, and the establishment of *ryū*. *Ryū* is best translated as 'school', in the sense of a continuing tradition, like the 'school of Rembrandt', rather than an actual building, for which the correct Japanese equivalent in martial arts terms is *dōjō*. One of the first *ryū*, that can be dated with some accuracy is the Shintō-ryū, otherwise known by its full title of the Tenshin Shōden Shintō-ryū. *Tenshin Shōden* means 'divine, true and correct tradition', and *Shintō* is the same word as the title of Japan's indigenous religion, which is usually translated as 'The Way of the Gods'. Its founder was Iizasa Chōisai Ienao, who was probably born in 1387 in a village called Iizasa in Shimōsa province, to the east of present-day Tōkyō. Near to Iizasa was a very important Shintō shrine, the Katori *jingu*, where was enshrined one of the most important deities associated with martial arts, Futsunushi no kami. During his youth Iizasa served the Shogun Ashikaga Yoshimasa, then returned to his home province, and after many spiritual experiences in the Katori shrine founded the school which exists to this day, hence the other name by which it is known, the Katori-Shintō-ryū. The date of the school's foundation can be placed in the mid fifteenth century, as Iizasa died in 1487 or 1488.

The founding of the Chūjō-ryū, second of the early schools, may well have occurred prior to the time of Iizasa's Shintō-ryū, but its early history is not clear, nor is there any definite account of the life of its traditional founder Chūjō Nagahide, who is supposed to have served the Shōgun Ashikaga Yoshimitsu. For this reason the Shintō-ryū is commonly given precedence, but whatever the origins of such schools, it is clear that by the beginning of the sixteenth century they and their offshoots were very active in teaching the families and the retainers of powerful *daimyō* (warlords) the niceties of

◄ **A *daishō* pair** The *katana* was slightly shorter than the *tachi*, and was designed to be carried thrust through the belt so that a blow could be delivered straight from the scabbard. This was not usually practical when wearing armour. This example is mounted with a *wakizashi* to make a pair of swords, or *daishō*. (Courtesy of Sotheby and Co.)

swordplay, a skill they had to master in the time of almost constant warfare that engulfed Japan after the Ōnin War.

Learning the sword

Sensei (teachers) such as Iizasa Ienao began a long tradition of education in sword technique, but they were of course hampered by one almost inescapable fact, that realistic practice with such a sharp and deadly weapon was almost impossible. The slightest mistake on behalf of one of a pair of sparring students would have led to a death, so various teaching methods were developed to

▲ **The first *sensei*** This illustration depicts Iizasa Chōisai Ienao, founder of the Tenshin Shōden Shintō-ryu, which is usually regarded as the first of the classic swordfighting schools of Japan. To the right of the picture appear two sorts of *bokutō*, wooden practice swords.

get round this problem. One was the practice of *suburi*, a drilling method whereby the sword was swung over and over in a form of 'shadow-boxing'. Alternatively the student could practise *kata*, a series of standard forms. When *kata* were practised with a partner each knew precisely what the other's next move would be. Both

LEARNING THE SWORD

suburi and *kata* were repetitious and boring, and required great dedication from the student.

Another form of practice was to substitute dummy weapons for real ones, and allow a certain amount of contact between opponents. For *yari-jutsu* (spear techniques) pupils used *tampo-yari*, a practice spear with a round padded end, and for swordfighting they used *bokutō*. The word *bokutō* consists of the two characters for 'wood' and for 'sword', because that is what *bokutō* were — wooden swords made with the overall shape of a real sword and with a real sword's approximate weight. To compensate the higher density of steel, the blade was made about one inch thick, and was practically identical with the modern *bokutō*, also called *bokken*, used in present-day *aikidō*. Instead of wearing armour, as is done in modern *kendō*, the *bokutō* fighters fought with unmasked faces and unprotected sleeves, so that even if mortal wounds and disablement were avoided, very

savage blows could still be sustained leading to severe bruising and the occasional broken limb.

Bokutō were also used for duels between rivals, as we shall see in a later chapter, and it was accepted practice that before two men began such a fight they exchanged documents which said that neither cared for mortal wounds. In some contests the fighters would use a method of pulling their punches before the opponent was actually struck, thus giving one a victory 'on points'. This technique, also used in practice, was called *tsumeru*, and was brought to perfection by Miyamoto Musashi, who,

▼ **A fight using *shinai*** An illustration from Hokusai's sketchbook depicting two samurai practising with what are probably *shinai*, the light bamboo swords used in modern *kendō*. They could however be *bokutō*, the heavier wooden practice swords.

THE TRIUMPH OF THE SWORD

according to one of the many stories told about him, could so control the blow from a real *katana* that he could sever a grain of rice placed on a man's forehead without drawing blood. To be praised for one's *tsumeru*, especially in the heat of a contest, was one of the greatest compliments a swordsman could receive. This, however, was always difficult to achieve (compare modern *karate*!), and as difficult to judge victory. This is very well illustrated in a famous scene in the film *Seven Samurai*. The duel is based on an incident that is supposed to have

occurred in the career of the swordsman Yagyū Mitsuyoshi, when the supposed loser in a fight with dummy swords is so convinced he has won that he makes his opponent fight with real swords, and is killed in the process.

Even during the Sengoku Period it did lead to rather odd-looking and unsatisfying contests. Some *sensei* selected only those pupils who were good at *tsumeru*, perhaps because of the damage unrestrained practice could produce, which was not perhaps the most appropriate criterion to apply in a situation where wars were liable to break out at any time. Towards the end of the sixteenth century *shinai* were developed for 'friendly' encounters. The *shinai*, the weapon used in modern *kendō*, which consists of a number of light bamboo blades tied together in a cloth bag, enabled what one

▼ **A fight with real swords** In this scene from *Seven Samurai*, which is based on an incident in the life of the swordsman Yagyū Jūbei Mitsuyoshi, two rivals prepare to fight using real swords, having failed to show a convincing result using wooden swords.

might term 'full-contact *kenjutsu*' to be practised, making a simulation of actual combat more realistic. It was introduced by Kamiizumi Nobutsuna, and first used by him in his meeting with Yagyū Muneyoshi, which we describe in a later chapter. A century later, in about 1711–1714, Chōshō Shiroemon of the Jikishinkage-ryū began to use protection for the face and forearms for practising martial arts, but they were always abandoned for serious contests, and *bokutō* used.

But if the *dōjō* gave little opportunity for realistic combat, there was no shortage of the real thing on the battlefield, and this is the theme we shall examine in the next chapter.

▶ **Equipment for *kenjutsu*** This *bokutō* and protective gauntlets are at the Maniwa Nen-ryū *dōjō*.

5.

The Lone Warrior in the Age of War

The Ōnin War of 1467 ushered in a century and a half of almost continual strife throughout Japan, which historians have dubbed the *Sengoku-jidai*, the 'Age of the Country at War'. With the collapse of Shogunal authority warlords called *sengoku-daimyō* fought with one another to increase their territories. Alliances were made and broken. New dynasties were created, while old ones disappeared forever. These were the days of large-scale strategy, huge battles, and tremendous developments in weaponry and tactics. Lower-class troops, the *ashigaru* (light-feet) who began as press-ganged peasants, came much more into prominence in the huge armies that were needed, and from the mid 1540s onwards, we read of firearms being used for the first time in Japanese history, though their full potential was not to be realized for three decades.

The graduates of the schools of *kenjutsu* discussed in the previous chapter put their skills to the test on the battlefield, where there was much fighting, but often little in the way of artistic sword technique. Nor was there much scope for the brave lone samurai, the lone warrior being less prized as an individual fighter than at any time in Japanese history. He was however prized as a leader. The great 'individuals' of the Age of War were men who commanded others, and set an example by the excellence of their fighting in the press of battle, rather than as samurai renowned for selfish feats of individual glory. The *Sengoku-jidai* was therefore the age of samurai armies, rather than of samurai, but now and again the individual spirit asserts itself, and there are a surprising number of examples of this happening, some of which we shall examine in this chapter. We shall also note the genuine, and perhaps slightly nostalgic pride that commanders took in their followers when this occurred, provided of course, that it did not interfere with the overall aim of the army.

The head of Yoshimoto

A particularly striking opportunity for individual glory presented itself at one of the most decisive battles of the Sengoku Period: the Battle of Okehazama in 1560, when the enemy commander's head was the prize. The background to Okehazama was that the up-and-coming warlord Oda Nobunaga had set out to confront the mighty host of Imagawa Yoshimoto, who were advancing into his territory, even though Nobunaga was outnum-

THE HEAD OF YOSHIMOTO

▲ **The death of Yoshimoto A rare opportunity for glory came the way of two samurai in Oda Nobunaga's army at the Battle of Okehazama in 1560, when they took the head of the enemy commander, Imagawa Yoshimoto. Battles of the Sengoku Period usually tended to be very anonymous affairs. (From the *Ehon Taikō-ki*.)**

bered by twelve to one. Scouts had told him that the Imagawa army were resting in a little gorge called Dengaku-hazama. As Nobunaga was operating on home ground it was an easy operation to lead 3,000 men on a circular route through the wooded hills to drop down in a surprise attack. Even the weather was on his side. It was a stifling hot day, and Yoshimoto's sentries were not at their most alert while Imagawa Yoshimoto performed the traditional ceremony of viewing the heads of the enemy they had killed on their way through the province. One by one the grisly trophies were paraded in front of

him, a label on the pigtail proclaiming the names of the victim and the noble samurai who had defeated him. Food was consumed, and the *saké* flowed freely, as Yoshimoto, dressed in an elaborate *yoroi* suit of armour, declared to his men that neither god nor demon dared to meet his army.

At about midday, as the surprise attack drew silently near, a terrific thunderstorm began, which cloaked Nobunaga's final movements. As the clouds blew away the Oda troops poured into the gorge of Dengaku-hazama. The Imagawa troops were so unprepared for an attack that they fled in all directions, leaving Yoshimoto's curtained field headquarters quite unprotected. Imagawa Yoshimoto had so little knowledge of what was going on that he drew the conclusion that a drunken fight had broken out among his men, and seeing an angry-looking samurai running towards him barked out an order for the man to return to his post. He only realized that it was

THE LONE WARRIOR IN THE AGE OF WAR

one of Nobunaga's men when the samurai, called Hattori Koheita, aimed a spear-thrust at him, but by then it was too late. He drew his sword and cut through the shaft of the spear, the blade continuing in a wide sweep to cut Koheita's knee, but before he could do any more a second samurai called Mōri Shinsuke grabbed him and lopped off his head. Not surprisingly, the Imagawa resistance collapsed at this point. The two Oda samurai became heroes, having participated in an almost unique event, that of finding for themselves the worthiest opponent of all. There had been no time for a challenge, but none would have been expected in the Sengoku Period. The overall aim of the battle had been carried out, and indeed enriched by their seizing of the opportunity, and that was honourable enough.

But such opportunities were few and far between, and even the greatest swordsmen of the day had to content themselves with a score of anonymous opponents rather than one who was noble and worthy in the tradition of their ancestors. Nothing better illustrates this than the early career of Kamiizumi Nobutsuna, the man who was to become known as one of the greatest swordsmen of Japan, but who, unlike the heroes of a previous age, had to leave the battlefield to achieve this distinction.

Kamiizumi Nobutsuna, the master swordsman

The career of the great swordsman Kamiizumi Nobutsuna is closely bound up with two important warlords of the Sengoku Period: Uesugi Kenshin and Takeda Shingen. The Uesugi territories stretched from the Japan Sea coast to the central mountains, where they met the Takeda sphere of influence in the neighbourhood of a rich flatland called Kawanakajima, an area that provided a battlefield for the two rivals on five separate occasions from 1553 to 1565. Apart from these five 'Battles of Kawanakajima' there were many other encounters between Uesugi and Takeda followers as each tried to take over the other's castles.

During the late 1550s Takeda Shingen allied himself with the powerful Hōjō family, and with their support set in motion a programme of taking all the Uesugi fortresses throughout the province of Kōzuke. The sequence of conquests proceeded smoothly until it came to the one farthest away from Takeda influence: Minowa castle, which was defended fiercely by a retainer of the Uesugi called Nagano Narimasa. For this reason Takeda Shingen

▼ **Kamiizumi Nobutsuna** Nobutsuna was a swordsman whose career spanned the whole range from the soldier fighting anonymously in battle, to the master of *kenjutsu*. A superb swordfighter in his own right, he is best remembered for being the founder of the Yagyū Shinkage-ryū, one of the foremost schools of swordfighting in Japan.

left it well alone, but in 1561 Narimasa died, and fearful lest the Takeda should take advantage of this the Nagano followers kept his death secret for as long as possible while his heir Narimori consolidated his position. He proved to be every bit as capable as his father, and had the advantage of the loyalty and fighting skills of a samurai called Kamiizumi Hidetsuna.

Kamiizumi Hidetsuna (Hidetsuna was his original adult name) was born in about 1520, the son of Kamiizumi Hidetsugu, keeper of Ogo castle in Kōzuke.

KAMIIZUMI NOBUTSUNA, THE MASTER SWORDSMAN

His father was a retainer of the Uesugi family, which meant that Hidetsuna's military career was to be bound up in the long rivalry between Uesugi and Takeda. Hidetsuna's swordfighting skills were a product of the third of the four outstanding traditions of swordfighting to emerge during the years of war, whose name we now add to that of the Shintō-ryū and the Chūjō-ryū. The Kage-ryū ('shadow-school') originated from a certain Aizu Hyūga-no-kami Ikō (1452–1538?), of whom little is known. Hidetsuna's father had been Aizu's pupil, and had passed on his knowledge to his son.

Takeda Shingen had no intention of allowing a long siege against Minowa castle. It had to be captured, which meant that in the hand-to-hand combat swordfighting skills would come into their own. Fortunately for all

concerned, fighting on foot was now a recognized and valuable component of samurai skill. Long or short straight-bladed spears had become common for samurai, but, helped by the new styles of suits of armour that allowed freer movement, the wielding of a sword had now become an integral part of samurai warfare.

There had also been many changes in armour during the previous century, spurred on by the longer duration of campaigns. It was no longer sufficient for armour to be lugged on to the battlefield in a box by a servant. It now had to be worn for days at an end. The *dō-maru* style was modified so that it had a definite waist, taking much of the weight off the shoulders and on to the hips, exaggerated in some cases to form the *okegawa-dō*, which was virtually a solid plate cuirass similar to contemporary European armour. The design of the *sode*, the shoulder plates, was also changed, reducing them considerably in size. Most recognizable, too, was a reduction in the number of cords which tied the armour plates together. Instead of the *kebiki-odoshi* style, of

---

▼ **Castle under siege** This modern reworking of an old print shows various handweapons in action at the Siege of Ōsaka in 1615. The combats at Minowa would have looked very similar.

THE LONE WARRIOR IN THE AGE OF WAR

numerous closely woven cords, *sugake-odoshi*, spaced out braiding, meant less weight, and a saving in time for busy makers of armour. A face mask was also introduced, which as well as protecting the face, served as an anchor point for the cords of the helmet. All in all, the armour of the Sengoku was a solid and practical battledress, giving the maximum protection and allowing the freest movement that current technology could provide.

We may therefore picture Kamiizumi Hidetsuna fighting fiercely with sword and spear at the rear of Minowa castle, with the young heir leading at the front. Attack after attack was repulsed, with the action almost totally involving hand-to-hand combat. Finally Hidetsuna took the fight to the Takeda and sallied out of the castle in a bold surge, leading the rush with his own swift and sharp sword. The Takeda became demoralized. They had been fighting, as distinct from merely besieging, for nearly a month, and their casualties were mounting. But then fate took a hand, for in another sally by the defenders the young heir Narimori was cut down and killed, and this time there was no opportunity to keep a commander's death a secret. The Takeda seized upon this huge psychological weapon. The heir to the Nagano family had died childless. There was no leader, and the shattered defenders were forced to sue for peace. One condition was that the relatives of Nagano Narimori be put to death, a demand commonly made in these circumstances, and the offer was made to incorporate the brave defenders of the castle into the Takeda army, again not an uncommon course of action.

Takeda Shingen, however, had a special honour in store for the brave opponent whose swordfighting skills and charisma as a leader had frustrated his efforts for a month. He allowed Hidetsuna to change his name to Nobutsuna, 'Nobu' being one of the characters in Shingen's own given name, Harunobu (Shingen was the name he had taken on becoming a monk). As the character *nobu* was hereditary within the Takeda family almost no greater honour could have been bestowed. He, however, declined the offer of service to Shingen, and explained that he wished to set out on a journey to improve his swordfighting skills, an activity that was becoming *de rigueur* among those who regarded themselves as master swordsmen. We will examine Nobutsuna's wanderings, and other examples of the 'warrior pilgrimage', in the following chapter.

The unexpected combat

The implications of the above story are that single combat during the Sengoku Period was a rare event. Kamiizumi Nobutsuna must have fought a hundred duels during the month-long defence of Minowa, but we know the names of none of his opponents. All were victims as anonymous as the Mongols slain in 1281 in the heat of battle, with no time to challenge a worthy opponent. Later in that same year of 1561, however, there was an encounter between two very worthy opponents, namely Uesugi Kenshin and Takeda Shingen, a single combat fought between two commanders, which happened almost by accident.

The Fourth Battle of Kawanakajima in 1561 was the fiercest battle fought between the Uesugi and the Takeda. The Takeda had advanced to Kawanakajima and reinforced their garrison at Kaizu castle. The Uesugi had advanced to meet them and had taken up a position on Saijoyama, which overlooked Kaizu from a distance. On three previous occasions there had been a stalemate between their armies, but this time Shingen had a plan, worked out by his *gun-bugyō* (Chief of Staff) Yamamoto Kansuke, who as well as being a strategist was also a noted swordsman and had produced a book about sword technique. A detachment of troops would climb Saijoyama from the rear by night, and attack the Uesugi positions. This would drive the Uesugi army down the north side of the mountain, across the river and into the waiting guns and sharp blades of Shingen's main body, who were to cross the river in secret and take up a battle formation in the centre of the flatlands of Kawanakajima, all under cover of darkness.

Both the Takeda and the Uesugi were skilled at using mounted samurai in a way very different from that of the Gempei War. No longer were they individual archers, but a well-organized cavalry arm, whose operations in the flatlands of central Japan had made them skilled at devastating charges, wielding from the saddle swords, *naginata* or long spears, which were swept from side to side, cutting down enemy footsoldiers. The best counter to such measures, which was the mass firing of arquebuses by the same footsoldiers, had still not been fully developed.

The operation began at midnight of the day selected. Takeda Shingen led 8,000 men out of Kaizu to the aptly named Hachimanbara ('War God Plain'). Unknown to

THE UNEXPECTED COMBAT

Shingen, however, Uesugi Kenshin had not been idle. His scouts on Saijoyama, or perhaps vigilant spies sent down to Kaizu, reported seeing fires in Kaizu, and signs that Shingen was making a move. Kenshin guessed what the plan might be, and planned a counter move, also to be carried out at dead of night. In total secrecy Uesugi Kenshin descended from Saijoyama by its western flanks, and charged down upon the Takeda army out of the morning mist.

Swinging their long spears from the saddle, the mounted samurai of the Uesugi crashed into the Takeda unit commanded by Takeda Nobushige, Shingen's younger brother and his second-in-command. Nobushige died in the fierce hand-to-hand fighting which followed. The Uesugi general Takemata Hirotsuna then led his followers against the veteran Takeda leaders Naitō Masatoyo and Morozumi Bungo-no-kami, and was knocked clean off his horse, the force of the blow as he hit the ground dislodging his helmet. As the fight

▲ **Spearman in action** This illustration from the *Ehon Taikō-ki* is reminiscent of the scene in *Seven Samurai* for its dramatic showing of the power of a mounted spearman against poorly defended footsoldiers, who are swept to one side by the force of the charge.

continued Shingen's *gun-bugyō* Yamamoto Kansuke realized that his carefully made plans had failed. He accepted full responsibility for the disaster which his error of judgement had brought upon them, and resolved to make amends by dying like a true samurai. Taking a long spear in his hands he charged alone into the midst of the Uesugi samurai, where he fought fiercely until, overcome by bullet wounds, and wounded in eighty places on his body, he retired to a grassy knoll and committed *hara-kiri*.

Meanwhile, Takeda Shingen, seated on his folding camp stool, was trying desperately to control his harassed army from his command post. But great danger was

52

THE LONE WARRIOR IN THE AGE OF WAR

at hand. The enemy had by now reached the Takeda headquarters troops and Shingen's personal bodyguard. Shingen's son Takeda Yoshinobu was wounded, and at this point there occurred one of the most famous instances of single combat in samurai history. According to the *Kōyō Gunkan* (the only written source for this incident) there came bursting into the curtained enclosure of Takeda Shingen's headquarters a single mounted samurai, wearing a white headcowl, and with a green *kataginu* (a form of surcoat) over his armour. It was Uesugi Kenshin himself! He swung his sword at Shingen, who did not have time to draw his own sword, but rose from his camp stool and parried the blows as best he could with his *gumbai uchiwa*, the heavy war-fan carried by generals, which he had been using for signalling. He received three cuts on his body armour, and took seven on the war-fan until one of his retainers, Hara Osumi-no-kami, came to his aid and attacked the horseman with his spear. The blade glanced off Kenshin's armour, making the spear shaft strike the horse's rump, which caused the beast to rear. By now others of Shingen's guard had rallied to their master's side, and Kenshin was driven off. There is an alternative tradition that it was not

▲ **Spear techniques from the saddle** This scene from *Seven Samurai* shows the use of the spear from the saddle as a cutting weapon rather than like the European lance. Mounted spearwork, in mass charges, was a speciality of the Takeda family until they met their match against volley firing of arquebuses at the Battle of Nagashino in 1575.

▶ **Sword versus warfan** One of the most notable single combats during the sixteenth century occurred between the two rival commanders at the Fourth Battle of Kawanakajima in 1561. Uesugi Kenshin led a surprise dawn attack on the field headquarters of Takeda Shingen. The raid was so sudden that Shingen was initially forced to defend himself with the warfan with which he had been directing his troops. This illustration is by Hokusai.

Uesugi Kenshin who fought the combat but one of his vanguard, a samurai by the name of Arakawa. Nevertheless, the incident is an excellent illustration of the opportunistic nature of single combat in the Sengoku Period, and the devastating effect of a well-organized cavalry charge that has surprise on its side.

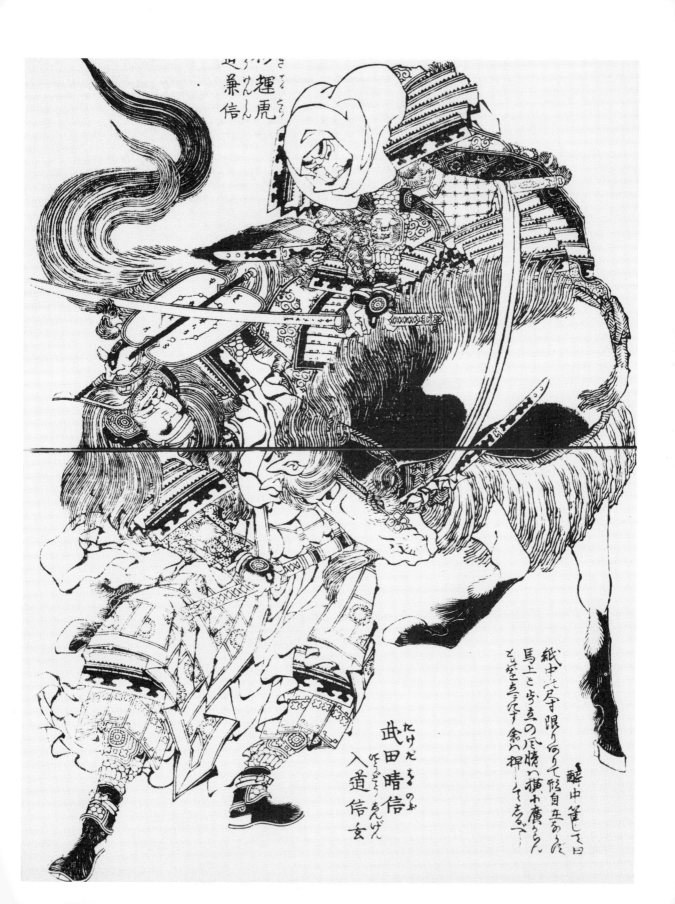

紙中六尺を限り向ひて
馬上と歩立の心懐ひ横ハ廣らん
と筆を三尺ニ余ハ押へて書る

ばしんひつして日

たけだ　ものぶ
武田晴信
しんげん
入道信玄

The wolf and the deer

Single combat during the Sengoku Period was not always anonymous or unplanned. In 1565 a certain Yamanaka Shika-no-suke fought a single combat in every bit as gallant a manner as had his ancestors of the Gempei Wars, and one for which both armies stopped fighting for a time to watch!

Yamanake Shika-no-suke was a retainer of the Amako family, whose territory was centred around the Inland Sea coast of the extreme western tip of the main island of Honshū. The Amako family's fortunes bear many of the hallmarks of the *sengoku-daimyō*. The Amako territory had been won by the sword, and was defended by a series of military actions throughout the middle of the sixteenth century. Their great rivals were the Mōri family, who besieged the Amako within their castle of Toda-gassan in 1565. Toda-gassan was a typical *yama-shiro* ('mountain castle'). It was built on a series of steep wooded hills overlooking the River Toda, making good use of the natural defences available. Yamanaka Shika-no-suke, as one of the leading retainers on the Amako side, took a full part in the operations. Shika-no-suke had been born on the fifteenth day of the eighth lunar month of 1545, the day of the harvest moon. He believed himself to be a heavenly child of the moon, as in the story of him in the author's *Samurai Warlords*, praying to the new moon, 'Grant and bestow on me the sevenfold troubles and the eight pains', and pledging to restore the fortunes of the Amako family.

Shika-no-suke dressed distinctively in a helmet with the crescent moon helmet crest and deer antlers (*shika* means 'deer'), and showed himself to be an outstanding fighter. This brought him to the attention of a certain Shinagawa Daisen, of the Mōri army, who took the unusual step for the times of issuing Shika-no-suke with a personal challenge. Daisen too was famous for his bravery, and was 'as fierce as a nursing mother tiger', according to one description of him, with superhuman strength. To provoke Shika-no-suke he announced that he was changing his name to Taraki Okami-no-suke, a complex jest aimed at his rival, because when the deer is eating the shoots of the *tara* plant its horns are lowered and the *okami* (wolf) can kill it.

The combat took place on an island in the middle of the Todagawa. A truce was proclaimed between the two armies, and several hundred sightseers gathered to watch the encounter between their champions. Okami-no-suke at first seemed inclined to settle the combat with an archery duel, and had fitted an arrow to his bow when it was taken from his hands, so the fight began with swords. Shika-no-suke cut Okami-no-suke with his sword, then grappled with him in a fight reminiscent of the *yoroi-gumi* contests of the Gempei War. Okami-no-suke wrestled him to the ground, but when Shika-no-suke was underneath him he wriggled out of his grasp,

▼ **The deer kills the wolf** The sixteenth century is not noted for the number of individual challenges to combat. One exception is the fight between Yamanaka Shika-no-suke and Shinagawa Okami-no-suke. Here the victorious Yamanaka takes his opponent's head using his *tantō*.

struck up with his *tantō,* and drove it up under the edge of his opponent's body armour. As Okami-no-suke fell dead Shika-no-suke cut off his head and shouted across the river, 'The deer has killed the wolf!'

This combat is a far cry from the sword duels shown in Japanese movies. It is a scrappy affair for something on which both armies seem to have laid such store, and one may take a cynical view that the interest taken in it was more to provide a little light relief from the tedium of siegework. But that was the nature of warfare during the Sengoku Period. Individual skills had to be exercised within the framework of the overall needs of the army, and the effects on morale of Yamanaka's victory probably justified the attention given to it. An equally dramatic account of individual heroism during a siege occurs in the chronicle *Ōu Eikyō Gunki,* which deals with events in the far north of Japan. The following vivid description occurs in the section dealing with the siege of Hataya Castle:

'The soldiers under the command of the general vied with one another in screaming and attacking furiously. Among them was a *hata-bugyō* in a scarlet-laced armour, and dressed in a crimson armour-robe. He had a *sashimono* with the character *jū* in black on a white field. He had more than thirty men under him, and attacked vigorously. About 100 *ashigaru* from Hataya castle tried to kill him. They opened the doors and shot out fighting furiously, then all of a sudden fourteen or fifteen men were killed and they were driven within the palisade. Here there was a man called Adachi Tōjurō of the Hataya headquarters. He waited inside the palisade and finally took the head of the general in the red costume who led the unit. This skilled man, who had more than thirty men under him, had become separated from his men under the great numbers of the castle garrison within the palisade, until he was alone, and was killed. Thereupon the general on the Aizu side, Miyabe Shūrisuke Yasunaga, launched an attack from three directions, blasting away from the muzzles of their guns, driving the defenders back to the edge of the ditch.

From within the castle two horsemen who gave their names as Watanabe Anzaemon and Yukii Genzaemon, who were of great merit, and both dressed in black laced armour and carrying *no-dachi,* advanced against the great host of the enemy.

They were forced to escape back inside the palisade, the gaps in their armour showing in red the many places were they had been pierced. "Let's go and meet the enemy general!" they shouted, and splitting up they entered the great army. Keeping unwaveringly to their determined purpose they attacked furiously as far as Miyabe's *hatamoto.* Watanabe mowed down Miyabe's page Satō Shūzen, killing him there and then. Yukii exchanged blows with Yasunaga, and was killed at that moment. Next the castle commander Goenojō, who was wearing a persimmon-coloured *katabira* (thin morning kimono) and carrying a hand spear, with his two loyal sons and sixty other superb horsemen, charged out as one, smashed into the enemy lines . . . fighting with the madness of death.'

The brave Makara family

The Battle of the Anegawa in 1570, fought between Oda Nobunaga and his brother-in-law Asai Nagamasa, was almost entirely a hand-to-hand affair. It was fought across a river, and among a remarkable number of single combats produced a series of actions fought not for individual glory but to cover a fighting retreat, placing the individual combat firmly in the mode of an action done for the greater good of an army.

At first it was almost as though there were two separate battles being fought: the Tokugawa against the Asakura, and the Oda upstream against the Asai. Both sides waded into the river, which was sluggish and about three feet deep, and fought furiously, the sweat pouring off them and mingling with the waters of the river which soon were stained with red. In an incident similar to the famous single combat at Kawanakajima, a certain samurai called Sasai Masayasu, armed only with a spear, fought his way to Asakura's headquarters, only to be blasted by a fusillade of arquebus fire.

At this point we read of another splendid exploit of samurai heroism, and from the opposite side. Honda Tadakatsu had launched his flank attack, which was so successful that Asakura Kagetake, the commander-in-chief, was completely surrounded in the furious mêlée. It was essential that the Asakura army withdraw to the northern bank, and a certain samurai called Makara Jurōzaemon Naotaka, a retainer of the Asakura, volunteered to cover their retreat. This Makara Jurōzaemon

THE LONE WARRIOR IN THE AGE OF WAR

was apparently a giant of a man, who carried a *no-dachi* sword with a blade more than five feet long. A *no-dachi* was normally swung with two hands, rather like the Scottish claymore, but Makara Jurōzaemon held his in one hand, and swung it from the saddle! Like the samurai of old, whose stories he would have been told as a child,

◀ **Sasai Masayasu at the Anegawa** Armed only with a spear, Sasai Masayasu fought his way to the headquarters of the enemy commander, and was blasted by a fusillade of bullets.

▼ **The bold Makara family** During the Battle of the Anegawa in 1570 Makara Jurōzaemon deliberately engaged the opposing army in a series of individual combats in order to give his own side the chance to regroup. He fought from horseback, and wielded a *no-dachi*, an extra-long type of sword. (From the *Ehon Taikō-ki*)

Makara bellowed out a challenge to anyone from the Tokugawa side who would come to fight him. His challenge was first accepted by a vassal of the Tokugawa called Ogasawara Nagatada, whom Makara killed.

He was then joined by his eldest son Makara Jurōsaburō Naomoto, and together father and son faced repeated attacks by Tokugawa samurai as the Asakura withdrew until both were killed. (See the author's *Battles of the Samurai* for a full account of the fighting.) But their sacrifice had not been in vain, because their rearguard action had allowed the army to rally, even though they were then pursued for a considerable distance. That put paid to the Asakura, but further upstream the Asai had reversed the positions, and another single combat took place. A samurai of the Asai called Endo Kizaemon had resolved to take Nobunaga's head, and had fought his way by hand-to-hand swordfighting into the headquarters post. He was only cut down, by a samurai called Takenaka Kyusaku, when he was quite close to his target.

The Seven Spears

The best evidence that the generals of the Sengoku Period valued individual fighting skills, and did not regard their samurai as a mass of anonymous cannon fodder, is the tradition of naming the seven most valiant warriors in a battle the *shichi hon yari* ('seven spears'). Thus we have the 'Seven Spears of Azukizaka', and best known of all the 'Seven Spears of Shizugatake'.

Shizugatake was a frontier fortress which belonged to Toyotomi Hideyoshi, and which was besieged by Sakuma Morimasa in 1583. Sakuma Morimasa led 15,000 troops, and ten hours previously had enjoyed a considerable success by capturing the fort on the neighbouring summit of Ōiwayama. But his commander, Shibata

▼ **The Seven Spears of Shizugatake** In this vigorous illustration some of the 'Seven Spears' charge along the mountain paths of Shizugatake, knocking Sakuma's troops to one side.

THE LONE WARRIOR IN THE AGE OF WAR

Katsuie's orders had been to attack only Ōiwayama, and withdraw inside it. He chose instead to disobey Shibata's orders and concentrate on capturing one further prize. That night Sakuma Morimasa looked down to see that a relieving army had arrived. He hurriedly changed his plans, and ordered his men to abandon their siege lines and take up a defensive position against Hideyoshi's attack, which was not an easy thing to do in the middle of the night on a densely forested mountain.

Leading Hideyoshi's vanguard was a young warrior called Katō Kiyomasa, eager to take part in his first major encounter. For Katō Kiyomasa the Battle of Shizugatake began with the sound of a conch shell, which ordered him into the attack against Sakuma's samurai. Wielding a cross-bladed spear, Kiyomasa confronted one of Sakuma's most experienced generals. Abandoning their spears for bare hands, the two grappled and the agile young Kiyomasa employed some *yoroi-gumi* or *jū-jutsu* techniques that turned the older man's strength against himself. The two samurai fell off the edge of a cliff, and Kiyomasa cut off the older man's head. Another young samurai, one year senior to Kiyomasa, who also distinguished himself at Shizugatake was Fukushima Masanori. He attacked a prominent samurai called Haigo Gozaemon and ran him through with his spear, the spear point entering Haigo's armpit and penetrating through to his stomach. Five more samurai earned great honour for themselves at the Battle of Shizugatake, and together with Katō Kiyomasa and Fukushima Masanori became known as the 'Seven Spears of Shizugatake'.

The nemesis of Nagashino

In spite of the achievements of the 'Seven Spears of Shizugatake', the tradition of the lone warrior on the battlefield was already rapidly becoming an anachronism. We have mentioned the sporadic use of arquebuses on the Sengoku battlefield, and the decisive blow in favour of these anonymous and inglorious weapons had been struck eight years prior to Shizugatake in the Battle of Nagashino, a turning-point in Japanese military history. Faced with the threat from the Takeda's renowned cavalry, and their devastating charges across open ground, Nobunaga constructed a loose palisade in front of his army, and lined up behind it 3,000 arquebusiers, trained, and sufficiently well disciplined, to fire in controlled volleys. The gunners were *ashigaru*,

▲ **Katō Kiyomasa performs yoroi-gumi** Katō Kiyomasa, one of the Seven Spears of Shizugatake, used grappling techniques against an enemy samurai until both fell off the side of a cliff, and Kiyomasa cut the other's head off.

lower class footsoldiers, who could easily be trained to fire the arquebus with all the accuracy of which the comparatively crude weapon was capable. The bow, the élite weapon of the samurai class, may have been more accurate, better ranged, and even cheaper to produce, but it took years of training and well-developed muscles to produce a good samurai archer, and in the furious years of the Sengoku Period time was in very short supply.

The Takeda cavalry were brought down in their hundreds, to be pounced on by samurai as worthy as themselves, wielding respectable swords and spears. But the damage had been done to the image of the lone warrior as an integral part of battlefield tactics. The attack by the noble could now be preceded by a devastating

Japanese vertical text in image.

▲ **Arquebuses in action** The arquebus, a matchlock musket light enough to be fired without a support, provided the counter to the mass cavalry charge.

bombardment from the ignoble. In a night attack such as Shizugatake the samurai could occasionally turn the clock back to a more glorious time, and armour could be made bullet-proof, but from Nagashino onwards prowess with the sword had to be sought elsewhere than on the battlefield.

The unwelcome combat

We conclude this chapter with an account of another swordsman whose career illustrates this point better than any other. Like Kamiizumi Nobutsuna, Ono Tadaaki was a great *sensei*, or sword teacher, who inherited the mantle of the Ittō-ryū, (which descended from the Chūjō-ryū) when his master Itō Ittōsai made Tadaaki and

another pupil fight a duel to become his successor. Tadaaki served the Tokugawa family as a *kenjutsu* instructor, and when war came he fought alongside his companions in the army. He was a member of Ieyasu's son Hidetada's army, the contingent that missed the Battle of Sekigahara because they were delayed along the Nakasendō road by laying siege to Ueda castle. The castle of Ueda was defended by the Sanada family, who realized the opportunity they had of splitting the Tokugawa army, and therefore allowing their ally Ishida Mitsunari time to destroy the main body. Consequently Ueda was defended more stubbornly than any similar siege, and in fact is regarded as one of the three classic sieges of Japanese history where the defenders were ultimately successful.

Ono Tadaaki held the position of *karita-bugyō*, or 'commissioner for harvested rice-fields', whose primary purpose was to ensure that crops were not looted. As there were other disciplinary functions it was a post that did not make the holder the most popular warrior in the army. It was a responsibility akin to being in charge of the military police. One day Tadaaki was making his regular tour of inspection when he saw a samurai approaching from the besieged castle, waving a spear and shouting what appeared to be a challenge. For a challenge to be shouted against a fortified line in the year 1600, where a hundred arquebusiers had their weapons trained on any happening, was an unusual event, and perhaps just one further example of the clever Sanada's delaying tactics, but the curious Tadaaki responded to the shout by heading over the line towards the challenger, closely followed by another samurai called Tsuji Tarō-no-suke. As the two samurai approached him the challenger thought better of his impetuosity, turned on his heels and fled, but as Tadaaki and his companion reached 'no-man's land' they discovered two other enemy soldiers who were obviously on a reconnoitring mission. The way they couched their weapons when they saw Tadaaki also convinced him that the two were good swordsmen. Sensing the opportunity of a rare occasion to display his skill, Tadaaki drew his sword.

Two individual combats therefore began. Tadaaki skill-fully parried the spearstrokes of his opponent, and felled him with the fourth blow of his sword. Had the man not been heavily armoured one might have expected the first blow to be fatal. His comrade in arms cut through the spear of his own adversary, whose nerve then cracked.

THE LONE WARRIOR IN THE AGE OF WAR

▲ **Sanada Yukimura** Together with his father Masayuki, Sanada Yukimura defended the castle of Ueda in 1600 against Tokugawa Hidetada, an action which kept a large number of Tokugawa troops away from the Battle of Sekigahara. It was the site of an unusual single combat fought between Ono Tadaaki of the besieging force, and a samurai from within the garrison. Tadaaki was later reprimanded for having broken ranks in search of personal glory, a strange reversal to popular ideas of the value placed on individual accomplishments. This statue is in the town square at Ueda.

He turned and fled, so the frustrated Tarō-no-suke contented himself with delivering a bad-tempered stroke to the already prostrate body of Tadaaki's foe, who, it was to be revealed, was a high ranking retainer of the Sanada called Yoda Hyōbu. Tadaaki and Tarō-no-suke withdrew to the lines under a barrage of arquebus fire, leaving the Sanada samurai to take away the body.

Now ensued a most unusual episode. Tadaaki reported the deed to his superior officer, only to find that Tsuji Tarō-no-suke had already reported that he himself had killed the man. So vigorously did each samurai argue his case that an inquiry was set up, and the claim seemed to hinge on identification, and whether or not the victim, who had worn red lacquered armour, was also wearing a facemask at the time. Tadaaki claimed that he was not, Tarō-no-suke said that he was. To settle the matter the Tokugawa hierarchy went so far as to send spies into Ueda to discover the truth about the dead man, and when they reported that he had indeed been wearing a face mask Tadaaki's story was vindicated. That was not quite the end of the affair, however, because Tadaaki, in pursuing the challenge, had broken ranks without permission for a private battle, and had therefore committed a breach of military law. Such a contrast to the days of the Gempei War! Tadaaki was found guilty and sentenced to a year's 'probation'. This was a strange end to an individual combat, but what is more remarkable is that none of Tadaaki's comrades spoke up on his behalf. Perhaps there was some resentment of Tadaaki because of his position as *karita-bugyō*, but perhaps there was also a feeling that to seek for individual combat was now counter-productive to samurai behaviour, and that Tadaaki's action, far from being admirable, was one to be condemned even by his fellow samurai, a neat reversal of the popular perception of single combat.

So what are we to make of the individual warrior in the Sengoku Period? To some extent the large-scale battles of the time gave as great a scope for individual swordplay as had the encounters of the Taira and Minamoto, despite the restrictions that the large-scale use of firearms placed upon it. The difference was that it could only rarely be conducted against a named opponent. Such personal challenges, unless they fitted exactly with the overall aims of the battle, were positively discouraged. This aspect of samurai behaviour was, however, not entirely dead, but it now had to be found off the battlefield rather than on it, and it is to this phenomenon that we now turn.

6.

The Wanderer

There is no more popular image of the lone samurai than that of the wandering swordsman, travelling from place to place, fighting duels, then wandering off again. For many people this wandering figure *is* 'the samurai', with the figure of the mounted archer, or the swordsman on the battlefield, as a dimly perceived shadow of reality.

This character has been personified most memorably to my generation by the great actor Toshiro Mifune in such films as *Sanjurō* and *Yojimbō*. Younger enthusiasts in Japan now follow the exploits in comics and television drama of the fictional character Itto Ogami, the 'Lone Wolf', who wanders the roads of Japan accompanied by his three-year-old son Daigoro, whom he pushes along in a wooden pram. His adventures sum up all the features of the archetypal lone samurai. He is ruthless, a superior

▲ **Lone Wolf and Cub** The fictional character Itto Ogami, the 'Lone Wolf', is the hero of a Japanese comic series. He is the archetype of the wandering samurai, personified two decades ago by Toshiro Mifune in films such as *Sanjurō* and *Yōjimbō*. He carries in his arms his infant son Daigoro, the 'cub' of the title. (Lone Wolf and Cub © 1989 First Publishing Inc. and Global Communications Corp.)

swordsman, and the victim of enormous wrong, which his never-ending and bloody journey seeks eventually to put right.

Itto Ogami, and most of the wandering characters Toshiro Mifune has portrayed, are *rōnin*, literally 'men of the waves', samurai who have no master to serve owing to the destruction of their clan in battle, the disgrace of their master, or personal dismissal. The 'Seven Samurai' in the famous film of the same name which is set in the year 1587, are all *rōnin*, and the long wars of the Sengoku Period meant that there was no shortage of dispossessed samurai seeking work for their swords. The background to *Seven Samurai* is therefore an accurate one, although most actual *rōnin* did not wander for long, but found employment with ease as *daimyō* competed with one another for good quality men to defend and expand their territories. It should be remembered, however that these are fictitious characters whose exploits and personal skills are often greatly exaggerated. The real 'wandering swordsmen' of history were often not *rōnin* with swords for hire, but *kengō* (master swordsmen) like Kamiizumi Nobutsuna, who chose voluntarily not to serve a particular master, and instead went on long pilgrimages to challenge worthy opponents and develop their skills as swordsmen. This was a form of spiritual and military training known as the *musha shugyō* ('warrior pilgrimage'). It was much akin to the common Japanese practice of making long religious pilgrimages to distant parts, thereby obtaining spiritual enlightenment through endeavor and personal discomfort.

Tsukahara Bokuden and the warrior pilgrimage

Probably the earliest recorded *musha shugyō* was performed by a certain Haneo Inno, a master swordsman of the Shintō-ryū, who lived between 1509 and 1579, but perhaps the most famous name from the early sixteenth century to become a wandering swordsman was the celebrated Tsukahara Bokuden, the first of the great *kengō*. There are few written accounts of his life, but a lively oral tradition tells us that he was born in 1490 in Kashima, in Hitachi Province. His father combined the professions of samurai and Shintō priest, the latter vocation being based at the Kashima *jingu*, where was enshrined the spirit of a god of martial arts. (Kashima, incidentally, is quite close to the Katori shrine which also enshrined a martial arts deity, and was the

cradle of the Shintō-ryū). It is therefore not surprising that the young Bokuden (or Takamoto as he was then named) was trained from an early age in swordfighting skills. His talent brought him to the notice of a swordsman of the Shintō-ryū who adopted the young man, and continued his training in the Shintō-ryū style. At the early age of seventeen Bokuden's adoptive father gave him permission to set out on a *musha-shugyō* pilgrimage, which was probably one of the earliest on record. It was very successful, and among those whom Bokuden defeated was a renowned swordsman called Ochiai. Bokuden spared his life, but it was such a disgrace to Ochiai to have been defeated by this young upstart that he lay in wait to murder him; on their second encounter he was killed by a rapid stroke of Bokuden's sword.

The area of Japan in which Bokuden lived suffered greatly from the interminable civil wars, and following his initial *musha-shugyō* Bokuden had to take his place in the armies of his lord, as did most of his contemporaries described in the previous chapter. We have no record of Bokuden's involvement on the battlefield, other than a note that he fought in thirty-nine separate engagements, and was involved in single combat nineteen times. He was apparently very good at singling out enemy commanders and killing them.

By the age of thirty-seven he had formed his own unique style of swordfighting, which he named Shintō-ryū. (The characters used for this Shintō are different from the Shintō-ryū of Iizasa, and mean 'new strike'.) Many pupils flocked to his side, but there were still those who sought to challenge him, among whom his biggest threat came from a man called Kajiwara Nagato, who was renowned for his wielding of the *naginata*. This was unusual for the Sengoku Period, as straight spears were the commonly accepted samurai polearm, but Nagato had trained for years with this fiercesome weapon. The great advantage possessed by a skilled *naginata* fighter over a swordsman was that his long polearm enabled him to attack the swordsman from beyond sword range. Bokuden began the duel by concentrating on the blade of the *naginata* as if it were a sword held by a man closer to him than was the case. Judging his distance carefully, Bokuden struck at the *naginata* as if he were cutting at this invisible opponent, and with his first stroke he sliced the shaft in half, leaving Nagato defenceless.

Bokuden called this decisive *i-ai* stroke delivered straight from the scabbard the *hitotsu-tachi* ('one-

TSUKAHARA BOKUDEN AND THE WARRIOR PILGRIMAGE

▲ **Tsukahara Bokuden** Tsukahara Bokuden was one of the first of the great *kengō*, or sword masters, and made three celebrated *musha-shugyō*, the warrior pilgrimage carried out by a swordsman to test and improve his skills by challenging worthy opponents. On his third journey he was accompanied by a large entourage, including followers flying hawks, as in this illustration from *Musha Shugyō Jun Rokuden*.

sword') implying in its meaning 'one stroke', and it became the hallmark of Bokuden's Shintō-ryū. As the Shintō-ryū was not destined to survive in the form Bokuden had begun we have no way of knowing whereof this devastating stroke consisted, but it served him well in building up a tremendous reputation. On his second *musha-shugyō* he was invited to Kyōto to teach *kenjutsu* to the Ashikaga Shoguns, the greatest commission any *kengō* could receive.

When he went on his third *musha-shugyō* he was attended by eighty followers, and took three spare horses. At the head of the procession he flew three large hawks, as proud as any *daimyō*. His procession was very splendid, but there was less of an air of ostentation about Bokuden himself, for he realized, as did all great swordsmen, that no matter how good he was he needed to pass on his skills to one trusted follower if his school were to survive, and this the warlike nature of the times finally prevented him from doing. It is believed that the essential secrets of the *hitotsu-tachi* were passed on to Kitabatake Tomonori, the *daimyō* of Ise province and his trusted pupil, who was charged with preserving the traditions and secrets, and initiating Bokuden's son into them when the boy was old enough. Tomonori did in fact pass them on to Bokuden's youngest son, whom his father had named as his heir, but when Bokuden died in 1571 at the ripe old age of 81 his successors became the

THE WANDERER

victims of forces far beyond the control of an individual swordsman. The Kitabatake suffered from the expansion into Ise Province of Oda Nobunaga, and Tomonori died defending his province. Accounts differ, and it is not clear whether he was killed on the battlefield or murdered by treacherous retainers. Nor is anything known of the fate of Bokuden's son, apart from a few fascinating legends about his joining the *ninja* groups of Iga.

Despite the lack of continuity, Tsukahara Bokuden remains a very important figure in the early history of the master swordsmen, and there are many stories told about him, of which the best is undoubtedly his encounter with a boasting samurai on a ferryboat. The man in question, who had managed to terrify the passengers with his bragging about his prowess at swordfighting, picked on the silent Bokuden, who alone had remained unintimidated, and challenged him to a fight. Bokuden

politely declined, saying that he never wielded his sword in such circumstances. The furious samurai poured scorn upon what he took to be cowardice, and asked Bokuden to name his school of swordfighting, to which Bokuden replied, 'the Munekatsu-ryū', ('the style that wins without a sword'). This reply made the samurai all the more angry, and he ordered the boatman to stop at a nearby island so that he could teach the stranger a lesson. As they reached the island's beach the samurai leapt ashore, and took up a guard position with his sword, screaming for Bokuden to disembark and fight him. At that moment Bokuden took the ferryman's pole and drove the boat away from the shore, leaving the samurai stranded. To the samurai's yells of protest Bokuden shouted back to him, 'See, this is what I meant by the Munekatsu-ryū! After all, I have just defeated you without a sword, haven't I!'

◄ **Tsukahara Bokuden and Miyamoto Musashi** The title of this print by Yoshitoshi tells us that it is of the aged Bokuden teaching swordfighting to the young Miyamoto Musashi. Musashi was in fact born twelve years after Bokuden's death, so such an incident can never actually have taken place. It would appear that the artist has mistaken Kasahara, a swordsman believed to have been Musashi's teacher, for Tsukahara. There are several prints by other artists where the name of Kasahara is correctly depicted. Musashi is shown with a long and a short *bokutō*, and Kasahara is receiving the blows on the wooden lid of a rice-pot. (Photograph courtesy of the Oranda-jin Gallery, Netherlands).

▼ **Saitō Denkibō** Saitō Denkibō was a pupil of Tsukahara Bokuden's Shintō-ryū, but exhibited none of the restraint associated with his teacher. In revenge for Denkibō's killing of his son in a duel, the father ambushed him in a temple, and he was shot down in a hail of arrows. (From the *Musha Shugyō Jun Rokuden*).

Saitō Denkibō

Apart from certain secret principles which a *kengō* wished to pass only to one successor, the wandering *sensei* (teacher) tried to ensure a good level of competence in all his pupils, and this did not always happen, either in terms of *kenjutsu* skills, or of acceptable behaviour. One of Bokuden's later pupils was a certain Saitō Denkibō Katsuhide, who was born in 1550. When he was twenty years old he went on a martial arts pilgrimage, and meditated in the great shrine of the war-god in Kamakura, the Tsurugaoka Hachiman-gu, where he had a dream of founding his own 'Tendō-ryū' school.

Eventually he went to the capital, where his reputation ensured that many novices were attracted to him and to the Tendō-ryū. He was a strangely flamboyant character, and wore clothes interwoven with feathers, so that people said he looked like a *tengu*, the goblins of the forests who were half man and half crow, and who had taught swordfighting to Yoshitsune. His conceit was like that attributed to *tengu* as well, which was quite unlike the calm nature of Tsukahara Bokuden, and there were many who were jealous of Denkibō and resented his boasting.

Among them was the fencing master of another school in Kyōto called the Kasumi-ryū, Shinkabe Aki-no-kami Ujimoto. Ujimoto thought Denkibō's conduct was scandalous, and totally out of keeping with the developing traditions of the *kengō*. Ujimoto's chief vassal had a son, a youth called Sakurai Kasumi-no-suke, who was Ujimoto's favourite pupil and was of some considerable talent. Those who resented Saitō Denkibō saw this young man as a potential champion for them, and tried to persuade him to challenge Denkibō, which flattery the naïve young man drank in. 'The Tendō-ryū are of no great consequence. Our Kasumi-ryū could defeat Denkibō with one stroke,' were the comments he heard. The remarks also came to Denkibō's ears, and, angry at this provocation, he challenged Kasumi-no-suke to a decisive swordfight.

Kasumi-no-suke was in a dilemma. He agreed to the fight, but thinking he would be scolded by the *sensei* Ujimoto for accepting a challenge, which was officially frowned upon, he kept silent about it, and arranged to meet Denkibō in a secret duel. There turned out to be a considerable difference between the talents of the two men, and Kasumi-no-suke was cut down with the single

THE WANDERER

hitotsu-tachi stroke that was the speciality of the Bokuden Shintō-ryū.

It was totally unnecessary to have killed the boy, but sadly typical of Denkibō's attitude. Kasumi-no-suke's father was furious when he heard of his son's death, and challenged Denkibō to meet him for revenge. 'Who is this old dotard, and what should I make of him?' scoffed Denkibō, as he set out for the contest, which was hastily arranged to take place at the nearby Fudō temple. However the grief-stricken father had not come alone and prepared only for a sword fight, but had brought ten soldiers with him. As Denkibō entered the courtyard he was met with a volley of arrows. He knocked aside with his spear up to three arrows fired at him, but the odds were against him, and he was mortally wounded by ten arrows shot through his body. He was thirty-seven years old.

Few contests between swordsmen were fought quite so bitterly as this one of Saitō Denkibō, and even the best-known 'wandering swordsman' of all often spared his victim's life. This was the famous Miyamoto Musashi, whose life has been so obscured by legend and fiction that it is difficult to disentangle the man from the myth. He comes over as a strange character, solitary and obsessive, whose skills with the sword were un-questioned and greatly admired, but which at the same time made him feared and disliked.

Miyamoto Musashi

Miyamoto Musashi was probably born in 1584, and led a life so full and eventful that he deserves a book to himself. To sum up the salient features of his life is difficult; we know that his appearance was marred by very bad eczema and he seemed to have an aversion to personal cleanliness. He seldom changed his clothes and almost never took a bath. By the age of thirteen he had become quite an accomplished swordsman, and at this age took part in his first *taryū-jiai*. The expression *taryū-jiai* means a duel between two individual opponents, but as the inclusion of the character *ryū* implies, the two opponents would be from two different schools of swordsmanship, the aim being to prove the superiority of a particular style, rather than that of a person. Musashi at thirteen had no school, of course, but was responding to a general challenge to *taryū-jiai* to all-comers from any school, which was issued by a certain Arima Kibei, a

swordsman of the Shintō-ryū. Musashi turned up for the duel armed with a *wakizashi*, the shorter of the two swords worn by samurai when out of armour, and a *bō*, the long wooden staff. It was the *bō* that he wielded against Arima's sword, and with it he knocked Arima cleanly to the ground.

In 1605 Musashi set off on a *musha-shugyō*, to fight some sixty authenticated duels over the following eight years. In Kyōto he defeated in two successive duels two brothers of the Yoshioka family, having first used a little psychological warfare by arriving late for each contest

MIYAMOTO MUSASHI

◀ **Miyamoto Musashi** A rather crude ink drawing of this illustrious but greatly feared swordsman. This simple caricature of him sums up the forbidding aspect he presented to many of his contemporaries.

▶ **Inei of the Hōzō-In** Inei was the Chief Priest of the Hōzō-In, a sub-temple of the Kōfuku-ji at Nara. He is carrying a *kama-yari*, the style of spear which he is credited with having invented when he was practising by cutting with his conventional straight spear at the reflection of the crescent moon in the waters of the pond of Sarusawa. (From the *Bukei Hyakunen Isshu*)

and thereby unnerving his opponents. He fought the elder with a *bokutō*, a wooden sword, and knocked him unconscious, breaking his right arm. The younger took up the challenge with a *no-dachi*, and Musashi killed him with his own normal *katana*. Disgraced by this reverse, the surviving Yoshioka issued a further challenge with real swords, but with a plan in mind similar to the revenge of Kasumi-no-suke against Denkibō. The scheme was that as soon as Musashi was engrossed in the duel the other Yoshioka followers would attack him *en-masse*, and avenge their previous reverses. But their tongues wagged a little too freely, and Musashi got to hear of the plot. So when he arrived at Ichijō-ji in northern Kyōto, the venue that had been selected, he was prepared for the sudden rush of swordsmen that descended upon him. The attackers were put off by his unexpected composure, and their careful plan went to pieces. One by one they fell beneath Musashi's sword.

Other opponents on his journey included a spearman from the Hōzō-In, a sub-temple of the Kōfuku-ji at Nara. The Chief Priest of the Hōzō-In, Inei by name, was a martial arts enthusiast, and it was said that he was never without a spear in his right hand. One night he had been exercising with his spear at dead of night, and was practising his moves by thrusting his spear at the new moon reflected in the waters of the Sarusawa Pond. The neck of the spearhead where it joined the shaft mingled with the crescent moon and took on the shape of a sickle. This gave him an idea to improve the design of a spear, and he fitted a crescent-shaped blade to the neck of the spearhead. This became known as the *kama-yari* of the Hōzō-In-ryū. The fame of the Hōzō-In, who used the *kama-yari* freely, gave these monks a fierce reputation, and Inei's pupil Shūji, hearing of the fame of Musashi,

challenged him to a contest. After some difficulty Miyamoto Musashi overcame the *kama-yari*, and emerged with a heightened respect for these fighting monks. A more serious contest was with a certain Shisido Baiken, who was adept with the *kusari-gama*, the weapon which consisted of a sharp sickle with a long weighted chain attached to the base of the handle. Musashi defeated him by throwing a small dart called a *shūriken*. This stopped the whirling of the chain, and then Musashi finished him off with his sword.

Musashi's most famous duel took place in 1612 when his wanderings brought him to Kyūshū, the large southern island of Japan. The foremost swordsman in northern Kyūshū was a man called Sasaki Ganryū, who served the Hosokawa family. Musashi's challenge to him was eagerly accepted, and they chose as venue the island of Funajima just off the mainland, which was later to become known as 'Ganryūjima'. Ganryū, a handsome and popular young man, made a great contrast to the disreputable-looking Musashi. Their choice of weapons, too, differed widely. Ganryū had his fine *katana*, Musashi just a rough wooden sword which he had whittled into shape from a boatman's oar. The duel, which was watched by hundreds of spectators, was a sensation. Both men appeared to land blows at the same moment, but it was Ganryū, not Musashi, who staggered from the

◀ **Miyamoto Musashi** A print of an actor playing the role of Musashi, the most famous 'lone swordsman' ever to have lived.

▼ **Toda Seigen** Toda Seigen was a swordsman of the Chūjō-ryū, and a retainer of the Saitō family of Gifu. He is famous for a duel he fought against a rival, whom he defeated using a piece of firewood instead of a *bokutō*. (From the *Bukei Hyakunen Isshu*)

force. He recovered, and slicing up with his sword, aimed a blow at Musashi, but Ganryū received another furious blow from the wooden sword, and fell dying. Without a word Musashi turned and walked back to his boat.

It is interesting to note that recent research has questioned Musashi's role in the duel with Ganryū. An article of November 1988 in the *Asahi Shimbun* quotes from a recently discovered manuscript which claims that Musashi was not alone when he challenged Ganryū, but was accompanied by several followers, and when Musashi knocked Ganryū to the ground he was only

stunned. The others then pounced upon him and killed him. This is very similar to the plot conceived against Musashi by the Yoshioka family, and calls into question the traditional image of Musashi as the supreme lone warrior. With the defeat of Ganryū, Musashi's first period of wandering ceased, and he opened a fencing school in Kyōto. This lasted until he became involved in the Ōsaka Campaign of 1614–15, and served on the battlefield. From this time on his life became a series of wanderings, short periods of service to various *daimyō*, numerous duels, and an increasingly deep philosophical insight into swordsmanship, taking its final form in the *Gorinshō* ('Book of Five Rings') which he completed shortly before his death in 1645.

Contests and conflicts

The above examples may give the impression that the *musha-shugyō*, far from being a spiritual journey, was nothing less than a series of killings, wasteful in terms of the obviously fine swordsmen who were killed. How could this possibly be justified, happening as it did at a time when every man was needed for the armies? The truth is that the vast majority of *taryū-jiai* and individual challenges never went to the death. In most cases the contestants did not use real swords and spears, replacing them by the wooden dummies used by students of martial arts for practising techniques in the *dōjō*. As we noted in an earlier chapter, these could produce very nasty wounds even in practice, and there was no shortage of injury when they were used for serious combat. An early example of a serious encounter using *bokutō* is the bad-tempered contest between Toda Seigen and a man called Umezubō during the 1560s. Toda Seigen was a famous *kengō* of the Chūjō-ryū, and a retainer of the Saitō *daimyō*. One day, apparently, Toda Seigen visited his family at Gifu, the Saitō headquarters. This was at the time when Saitō Yoshitatsu was keeper of Gifu Castle, and just before he lost it to Oda Nobunaga.

The Chūjō-ryū were not the only prominent school in those parts. The Saitō had another retainer, a person called Umezubō, who was a strong man, and a *kengō* of Bokuden's Shintō-ryū, of which fact he was very proud. In his opinion the Chūjō-ryū had a style of swordsmanship that was 'provincial', and that if challenged would be unlikely to win. A master of the Chūjō-ryū had now turned up on his doorstep, so he challenged Toda to a

THE WANDERER

contest to determine their superiority. The *daimyō* Saitō Yoshitatsu was in two minds over the matter. Could he afford to let two of his retainers fight among themselves, when there were powerful enemies outside who threatening the entire family's position? To set against that was the need for Umezubō's destructive arrogance to be curtailed. For a contest to take place, and him to be worsted without serious injury, was the most likely way of doing that successfully. But he eventually decided that the needs of the whole domain were paramount, and that the former course of action would be correct, so he entreated Umezubō to withdraw the challenge. But this only made Umezubō worse, and he accused Saitō of being frightened of the contest. That settled the matter. Saitō's own pride was now involved, and he accepted the challenge, ignoring his overlord's opinion.

On the appointed day the angry Umezubō turned up with a real sword, while Toda Seigen had only a *bokutō*. Nothing perturbed, Toda Seigen invited Umezubō to use the real sword against him, claiming that his *bokutō* would be quite sufficient against an opponent with a real sword. Such a confident gesture unnerved Umezubō, who put his real sword to one side and took a *bokutō* of his own. At this Seigen used a further psychological ploy and abandoned his *bokutō* in favour of a tree branch from a pile of firewood which was at hand! So the strange contest began. Using the tree branch Toda Seigen guided Umezubō's stroke as he brought the *bokutō* down in a sweep for Seigen's forehead. As the *bokutō* continued to the floor he stamped his foot down on it, breaking it in half. Umezubō unsheathed his *wakizashi* which, according to the custom of the times, he had not abandoned along with his real *katana*, and struck at Seigen, but Seigen dodged, and hit him with the tree branch, knocking him down. The one-sided contest was over in an instant, and Umezubō was thoroughly defeated and disgraced, but as it had been achieved without bloodshed the cohesion of the Saitō domain remained undisturbed.

The abuse of the challenge

Toda's fight, no matter how bad-tempered, was at least fairly challenged. There were, however, occasions when such challenge matches were excuses for bullying, and even theft. Whereas it was common for expert swordsmen such as Miyamoto Musashi and Tsukahara Bokuden

► **The Maniwa Nen-ryū dōjō** The Maniwa *dōjō*, which is still used for martial arts practice.

to travel the country seeking to have their skills tested and improved, others did it for personal gain, bringing disgrace upon what was originally a noble and chivalrous concept. Such ruffians would haunt a local *dōjō* hoping to pick on some unsuspecting pupil. This practice, called *dōjō-yaburi*, was common in the years between the campaigns of Sekigahara and Ōsaka (c.1601–14), and a surplus of unscrupulous *rōnin*, who were men of talent in swordfighting, pushed their way by their boasting into the *dōjō*s of many areas. They coerced others into fights, and made contests for bets, taking *saké* or cash as prize money.

The great swordsman Iwami Jūtarō tells of one *dōjō-yaburi* in his diary. In 1614 he set out on a journey for Omi on the north sea road, and intended to cross by boat from Nagahama to Otsu, but as the wind had dropped, he called in on an acquaintance, a village headman called Taira Zaemon. Zaemon's son Taira Saburō had received a wound on his forehead, and he told Jutarō how, on his way to the Itto *dōjō*, he had been challenged to a contest by the self-styled 'Seven *tengu*', a gang of men skilled at the martial arts, but apparently bullies and thieves. The leader of the *dōjō* was absent at the time, and no senior person was there to prevent such an abuse. The naïve young man had accepted the challenge from the ruffians, and was injured. He reported that the weapon with which he was wounded was a *bokutō*.

Jūtarō inspected the wound, and was certain that Saburō had been cut by something made of metal. Perhaps the gang members used *bokutō* made heavy by being reinforced with iron? Jutaro got very angry, and set off for the Itto *dōjō*. The 'Seven *tengu*' were still there, and appeared to be plotting to steal money and valuables. It turned out that their leaders were two very strong men who trained with metal weapons made to appear like *bokutō*, and with them they severely wounded opponents who used real *bokutō*. Jūtarō therefore knew that the weapon that would be wielded against him only looked like wood. Thus prepared, the splendid Jūtarō

► **Interior of the Maniwa Nen-ryū dōjō** The floor of the *dōjō* is of highly polished natural wood. Most of the old *dōjō*'s, the scenes of many *dōjō yaburi*, would have looked like this.

THE ABUSE OF THE CHALLENGE

THE WANDERER

▲ **The image of the lone samurai** A superb illustration from the *Ehon Taikō-ki*.

took them on and managed to beat them all. This is Iwami Jūtarō's narrative, which illustrates the reality of life in samurai Japan from the later Sengoku Period to the beginning of the Edo, when *dōjō* gangs swaggered about. But there could be a less sinister meaning to the phrase *dōjō-yaburi*, meaning serious but fair challenges from wandering swordsmen who visited a *dōjō* to seek out others to fight. Miyamoto Musashi's challenges have been called *dōjō-yaburi*, and here the word does not have the perjorative connotation outlined above.

By the later Edo Period about two hundred schools of martial arts were in existence, and among them were some *dōjō* masters of unusual talent. Many people wanted to challenge them, which led to a revival of *taryū-*

jiai and *dōjō-yaburi*. However, from the middle of the Edo Period only certain types of contests had been allowed, and to control them practice times and places were regulated. Within this framework contests were frequently encouraged, and some *sensei* ordered their pupils to take part. But there are also records of fights being fixed, or bribes changing hands as a money-bag was slipped into a sleeve, thus avoiding a contest! By this time, however, the martial arts were beginning to acquire the non-military ethos of today, and the resulting *dōjō-yaburi* was of a different nature. *Kenjutsu* was no longer confined to samurai but had spread to the lower classes. Chiba Shūsaku, a celebrated swordsman of the later Edo Period, whose career we shall study later, used *dōjō-yaburi* as a means of polishing his skill in a similar way to that of earlier times. In his lecture 'Kempō hiketsu' he lays out the rules for *taryū-jiai* contests between schools:

'When rival schools meet, there is sufficient fear in excited eyes and tightened shoulders, and in contrast to this, one approves of a spirit of gentleness and calm. There is a certain time when a man challenges someone to a contest, and everything in his body is humble. Think of our fellow students who are inexperienced in *kenjutsu* . . . do not despise anyone sent to the contest, think of them as skillful . . . receive them and allow for their behaviour, strong or weak.'

He adds that the greatest danger comes from the unknown adversary.

A wanderer founds a school

The swordsmen described so far in this chapter, especially Tsukahara Bokuden and Miyamoto Musashi, succeeded in their primary purpose in wandering because they developed their skills and their spiritual insight to the maximum extent. However they were lone wolves, and never managed to pass these skills on to others in any permanent form. We will cover the aspect of passing on traditions of *ryū* in the chapter which follows, but let us first examine the wanderings of a man whose distinguished career on the battlefield was followed by a pilgrimage, and the founding of one of the most illustrious swordfighting *ryū:* Kamiizumi Nobutsuna.

In the previous chapter we described how Nobutsuna was honoured by Takeda Shingen, but chose the wandering life instead of continued service to a *daimyō*. He set off on the *musha-shugyō* some time subsequent to 1561, and was accompanied on his travels by two companions, his nephew Hikita Bungorō, and Jingo Muneharu, each of whom was a renowned swordsman. One incident that occurred on his travels has become very famous owing to Akira Kurosawa's incorporating the story of it, with some modification, as a scene in the film *Seven Samurai*. On approaching a certain village Nobutsana was told that a criminal was holding a child hostage in a house. No one knew what to do, and the parents were desperate. Nobutsuna formulated a bold plan. He called over a priest, and asked if he could borrow his robe. Then, out of sight of the cottage where the child was being held, he had his head shaved. In his disguise as a priest Nobutsuna approached the cottage with two balls of rice in his hand. He explained to the

▲ **Hikita Bungorō** Hikita Bungorō was the nephew of the renowned Kamiizumi Nobutsuna, and travelled with him on his *musha-shugyō* pilgrimage. He is carrying the prototype *shinai*, with which he defeated Yagyū Muneyoshi. (From the *Musha Shugyō Jun Rokuden*)

THE WANDERER

criminal that he was a priest who had brought food for the child, and threw one of the rice balls through the doorway. He took the second rice ball, and, offering it to the criminal, rolled it along the floor towards him. The criminal grabbed at the rice ball, letting his guard down just for a second. At that moment Nobutsuna seized him in a *jū-jutsu* hold and pinned him to the floor. In the film the supposed priest kills the man with the man's own sword, but in the original version Nobutsuna tackled the swordsman and left him, quite unharmed, to the far from tender mercies of the villagers.

In 1571 Kamiizumi Nobutsuna received an honour that was probably without precedent for any swordsman, even a *kengō*. He was commissioned to demonstrate his skills before the Emperor Ogimachi (1521–73), who apparently loved *kenjutsu*, and was so impressed by Nobutsuna's performance that he granted him noble rank. But Nobutsuna's most important encounter of his journey was that with the man who was to become the heir to his tradition of swordfighting which he was now calling the Shinkage-ryū (*Shin* means 'new'). His opponent was to be Yagyū Muneyoshi, a man who, like Nobutsuna, had seen much service in battle, and was well known as a master *kengō*, having studied swordfighting under the Chūjō-ryū.

Nobutsuna and his companions had been given a letter of introduction to the monk Inei, Chief Priest of the Hōzō-In temple of Nara. Inei was related to the Yagyū. Knowing the reputation of both men, he decided to bring them together, and a contest was arranged to take place at the Hōzō-In. Nobutsuna was then fifty-five years old, while Muneyoshi was twenty years younger. We can imagine Muneyoshi's disappointment then, when he learnt that his opponent was not to be Nobutsuna himself, but his nephew Hikita Bungorō. A further surprise awaited Muneyoshi when he arrived, because Bungorō was not carrying a *bokutō*, but what appeared to be a bundle of bamboo sticks bound together – the first time anyone had seen the soon-to-be-familiar *shinai*. Muneyoshi faced his rival holding his *bokutō*. Each watched the other, waiting for an unguarded moment. Then suddenly Bungorō

struck, and Muneyoshi had the unfamiliar experience of feeling a wooden sword blade actually strike him across the forehead. Being used to *tsumeru* techniques he ignored the blow, and continued the duel, only to receive the *shinai* again. At this point Muneyoshi realized that he had come across a style of swordfighting superior to his own, and was about to acknowledge this when the master Kamiizumi Nobutsuna took the *shinai* from Hikida Bungorō and challenged Muneyoshi to a further duel. Muneyoshi took his guard, but the mere gesture of the challenge had beaten him. He threw his *bokutō* to the ground and knelt before Nobutsuna, begging to be taken on as his pupil. At that moment was born the Yagyū Shinkage-ryū, the greatest school of swordsmanship that Japan was ever to see.

▶ **Yagyū Muneyoshi** Muneyoshi was the first member of the Yagyū Shinkage-ryū, the most illustrious school of swordsmanship in Japan. The Yagyū became tutors to the ruling Shogunal family in Tokugawa. This is a wooden statue of him. (Kyodo News Agency)

7.

The Teacher

A very important factor in the development of the Japanese martial arts was the establishment of *ryū* around a charismatic personality of a master, who was often referred to as a *sensei* (teacher). We discussed the example of Iizasa Ienao in an earlier chapter, and the sixteenth century was to see the appearance of many others. Some, like Kamiizumi Nobutsuna, began as individual swordsmen in armies, or as 'child prodigies' like Tsukahara Bokuden and Miyamoto Musashi. Several of the most celebrated *kengō* managed to pass on their skills to others in their families in a permanent form, thus founding their own *ryū*. Many of these also became *sensei* to others outside the immediate circle of the *ryū*, some even achieving the distinction of sword instructor to the Shogunal families. To be referred to as *sensei* was a great honour, implying not only the quintessence of skill, but an almost un-challengeable status, making them the ultimate 'lone warriors'.

The great *sensei* thus became the most influential people in the development of the martial arts of Japan. All had their own individual characteristics and personality, and their own distinctive styles and philosophies, but by the very nature of the respect their position engendered, they all had two things in common – an aura of mystique, and a tremendous authority. Some acquired a hereditary position with a particular *daimyō*, while others maintained their own independent schools, and enjoyed the spectacle of swordsmen skilled in their own right begging to be allowed to be taken on as pupils. Such masters could therefore afford to be very selective about the people they chose to join them, and had very subtle ways of weeding out whom they wanted.

The ultimate pupil

We noted in the previous chapter that Tsukahara Bokuden had been tutor to the Ashikaga Shoguns. Such a commission from a Shogun was of course the ultimate accolade, and not one that a *sensei* either could, or would, decline. The ill-fated family of Ashikaga ruled Japan as Shoguns from 1333 until 1573, but its later members have often been represented as mere pawns in a power game, hopeless to stand up against the new *sengoku-daimyō* who ruled petty kingdoms of their own, heedless of Shogunal authority. At the level of politics this is probably true, but the Ashikaga family produced at

THE TEACHER

least one skilled swordsman in the person of the thirteenth Shogun, Ashikaga Yoshiteru. He was the pupil of Tsukahara Bokuden, who became his tutor in 1552 when Yoshiteru was seventeen years old. He was a promising pupil, and his skills were put to their ultimate test in 1565, when Matsunaga Hisahide and Miyoshi Chōkei, through whom Yoshiteru had been forced to rule as a 'puppet Shogun', determined to get rid of him.

Yoshiteru was at the time in his palace on Muromachi Avenue in Kyōto. In the middle of the night the palace was raided under the direction of the two conspirators. The guards proved useless. Most were in the pay of Miyoshi and Matsunaga anyway, and soon Yoshiteru found himself surrounded on all sides. Guns were discharged into the room as Yoshiteru drew his sword and prepared to put into operation the skills that Bokuden had taught him. His enemies appeared first only as dark shadows on the panels of the *shōji* that divided room from room. Sweeping the *shōji* to one side to reveal his

▲ **Practice in the dōjō A** *sensei* **looks on as his pupils practise under his supervision. (From the Hokusai sketchbooks)**

adversaries Yoshiteru laid about him with the sword, using the *hitotsu-tachi* strokes of the Shintō-ryū, but a spearman among them thrust at his legs and brought him to the ground. Mortally wounded by swordstrokes Yoshiteru crawled into another room and committed *hara-kiri*, a further noble gesture giving lie to the commonly held view of the weak and effeminate Shoguns.

The Tokugawa Shoguns, who followed the Ashikaga after a gap of about thirty years, were of very different political calibre, and the honour of teaching this dynasty fell to the two schools of the Ittō-ryū and the Yagyū Shinkage-ryū, who inherited Kamiizumi's Shinkage-ryū. We will deal with the Yagyū first.

THE ULTIMATE PUPIL

▲ **Death of the Shogun** Tsukahara Bokuden was tutor to the Shogun Ashikaga Yoshiteru. His pupil put his lessons to good effect when he was attacked by samurai of the conspirators Miyoshi and Matsunaga. The sword techniques were however not sufficient to save his life against enormous odds, and he committed *hara-kiri.* (From *Samurai Warriors*)

The Yagyū were a minor *daimyō* family with lands in the vicinity of Nara, and in the mid fifteenth century they were embroiled in the struggles for territory and power that went on in this part of Japan as much as it did elsewhere. Yagyū Muneyoshi participated in his first battle at the age of sixteen, which was fought against Tsutsui Junshō, an ally of Miyoshi Chōkei, the man who was eventually to murder the Shogun Yoshiteru. The Yagyū were defeated in the struggle and made to fight for the victor from then on, until Miyoshi's ally Matsunaga launched an attack on Tsutsui and the Yagyū joined

Matsunaga's side. Matsunaga was victorious, so the Yagyū subsequently fought for him. Their battles included one against warrior monks during which Yagyū Muneyoshi received an arrow through his hand, which does not seem to have affected his swordfighting prowess.

A few years later came his meeting with Kamiizumi Nobutsuna, and the beginning of the Yagyū Shinkage-ryū. The next most important event in the life of the Yagyū was in 1594 when Tokugawa Ieyasu invited Yagyū Muneyoshi to his mansion in Kyōto. Muneyoshi was accompanied by his son Munenori, and they gave such a display of swordsmanship that the enthusiastic Ieyasu took a wooden sword to try his skill against Muneyoshi. He brought the *bokutō* down against Muneyoshi's forehead, then before he knew what had happened, Muneyoshi had dodged, deflected the blow and grabbed the sword by the hilt in a move similar to the modern *kata* of *aikidō.* He held Ieyasu by the left hand and made a symbolic punch to his chest. The sword had gone spinning across the room. This was Muneyoshi's demonstration of the technique he called *muto*, literally 'no sword'. Following this encounter Ieyasu asked the Yagyū to become the Tokugawa's sword instructors. Muneyoshi excused himself on the grounds of his age, but suggested that his son Munenori would make an excellent *sensei*, an offer that Ieyasu gladly accepted. Muneyoshi then

▼ **Dodging the sword** A technique drawn by Hokusai, similar to the description given of Yagyū Muneyoshi's demonstration of his skills before the future Shogun, Tokugawa Ieyasu. These movements are now practised in *aikidō*.

retired from swordsmanship, and eventually died in 1606, by which time their pupil Tokugawa Ieyasu had become Shogun.

Munenori continued serving the Tokugawa to the third generation Shogun Iemitsu, but on the death of Muneyoshi the *ryū* split into two. His elder son, Munenori's brother, had been severely wounded in battle in 1571 and crippled so badly that he was unable to wield a sword, but as his was the senior line Muneyoshi passed on to the elder brother's son Toshiyoshi the official inheritance of the Owari Yagyū Shinkage-ryū, which was to serve the junior branch of the Tokugawa based in Nagoya. The school of Munenori, *sensei* to the Shoguns and based in Edo, became the Edo Yagyū Shinkage-ryū, which he eventually passed on to his son

PASSING ON THE TRADITION

Yagyū Jūbei Mitsuyoshi. There was much rivalry between the Edo and Owari schools over the years to come.

Yagyū Jūbei Mitsuyoshi is a character almost as mysterious as Miyamoto Musashi, and his adventures, which allegedly included spying and *ninja*-like activities, have spawned many historical novels and films. Most of the legends and inventions revolve around a 'lost' twelve years in his life, when he was abruptly dismissed by the Shogun, and later reinstated. His sacking was supposedly for drunkenness, but the lack of evidence, and the complete mystery surrounding his subsequent movements, has led many story-writers to the conclusion that his dismissal was merely a front. Mitsuyoshi then continued to serve the Tokugawa as a *ninja*, obtaining information for them as he went from province to province on a *musha-shugyō*, trying to wipe out his disgrace by worthy challenges. The best-known story about his wanderings was mentioned in a previous chapter. This is the incident with dummy swords re-enacted in *Seven Samurai*, whereby Yagyū Jūbei had to kill his opponent to convince him that he had actually won the contest by using *tsumeru* techniques.

The Yagyū family also play a strange part in the fictional adventures of Itto Ogami, the Lone Wolf, where they are portrayed as the villains of the piece, whose plotting forces the hero out on to his long and lonely journey.

Passing on the tradition

The history of the Yagyū family and their *ryū* is an excellent illustration of the procedure and beliefs that lay behind the means of passing on the secrets of a *ryū*, granting the right to teach and of choosing a successor. Passing on the inheritance of the mastership of the *ryū* was of course a very serious matter. Ideally the recipient would be a son, but if there were no child it could be given to another, the highest pupil. If subsequently a child were born it would be returned to the family, as in the case of Tsukahara Bokuden.

The various *ryū* of swordsmanship always claimed to possess their own specific and secret traditions. These secrets, the *menkyo-kaiden*, or 'secrets of the art' were known only to very few people in any *ryū*, who maintained the monopoly of this secret knowledge. Yagyū Munenori, Muneyoshi's heir, expressed it in the following way, in his preface to the *Heiho Kadensho*:

▲ **The cut stone** The strangest legend about Yagyū Jūbei Mitsuyoshi is that he cut this rock in half with his sword. It is near Yagyū village, and was probably split by lightning. Mitsuyoshi is one of the most mysterious characters in the history of the great swordsmen, and his life has spawned many novels and stories. He is supposed to have been a *ninja* for part of his life.

'The contents of those three volumes must not be released outside this family; however, this does not mean that our Way has to be completely concealed. To withold the prescribed skills and theories in our *ryū* means to preserve the purity of our tradition, and to transmit them to students who are truly qualified. If these are never transmitted to others, then it as if I had never written.'

In this treatise Yagyū Munenori uses the words *ie* ('family', or 'household') and *ryū* almost interchangeably, in a way that implies that he saw his students as his own children. In this extended family system the eldest son did not necessarily have precedence on inheritance. Although Munenori had inherited the Edo Yagyū Shinkage-ryū from his father Muneyoshi, he still pointed out that the successor to the head of the school was required to be the best-qualified student.

'The first volume of this book was called *Shinrikyo*, and outlined the entire contents which were directly

THE TEACHER

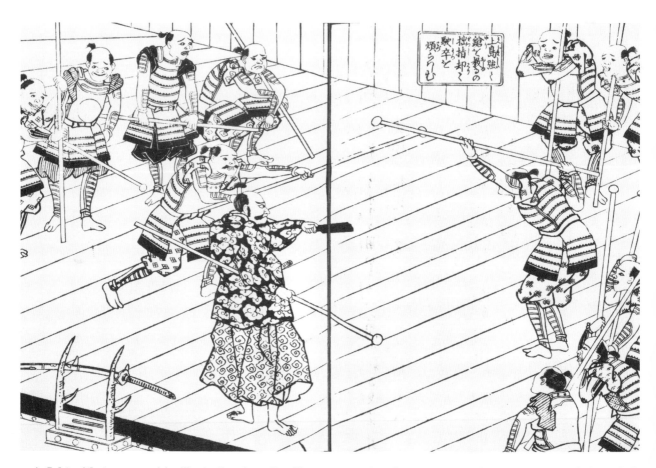

▲ **A fight with *tampo-yari*** An illustration from the *Ehon Taikō-ki* showing a contest between spearmen using practice spears.

transmitted to my deceased father from its founder Kamiizumi Nobutsuna. Nobutsuna's swordsmanship was compiled into one volume to preserve his knowledge by transmitting it to the student who strove to reach the highest.'

Muneyoshi gave Munenori, as Nobutsuna had given Muneyoshi, a certificate in the form of a scroll formally transmitting the secrets of the craft.

Not all knowledge was so esoteric. There were in fact three grades of 'secret': the *kirikami*, the *mokuroku* and the *menkyo-kaiden*. Broadly speaking they are analoguous to *dan* or teaching grades in modern *budō*, but at a much higher level. *Kirikami* dealt with the funda-

mentals of posture and the preparation of the mind, which was the basis of their techniques. A more mature person who had studied more deeply would receive the *mokuroku*, which indicated a certain insight on behalf of the pupil. Last of all, and the highest was the *menkyo-kaiden*.

To form one's own *ryū* was the final stage of the three which some *sensei* identified as being the path of instruction, expressed by three characters pronounced in Chinese. The first was *shu* ('to keep, observe or obey'), which had as its goal to copy perfectly the techniques taught by the *sensei*. The second was *ha* ('to break'), indicating that the student was now ready to apply these techniques, adjusting them if necessary, thereby developing his own style. The final stage was *ri* ('to depart') whereby a student finds new techniques, and ultimately creates an entirely new style of his own. This, however, was a very rare event during the Sengoku Period. One example is Marume Kurando, a pupil of Kamiizumi Nobutsuna, who originally disgraced himself during Nobutsuna's absence by ignoring the *sensei's* ruling banning contests, and taking on in a spear fight a man called Otaki Shigoroemon, whose nose Kurando cut off. Kurando was punished for this, but from that time on he worked hard at his training and eventually became one of Nobutsuna's star pupils. In 1567 Kurando asked Nobutsuna for the *menkyo-kaiden* of the Shinkage-ryū, which was presented to him as a scroll which still exists. Part of the text reads: 'Having instructed so many in the virtues of strategy in many provinces, since you are first in the ability of strategy . . . you will be initiated into the secrets. The mystery of the two swords has not been taught except to one person in the whole country. This must be kept absolutely secret. In consequence I give this letter my seal.' As Kurando could not be Nobutsuna's heir he went back to his native Kyūshū, and founded the Taisha-ryū, which become for many years the official *kenjutsu* school for the Shimazu family of Satsuma. He died in 1627 after a full and long life.

In addition to passing on one's own *ryū*, or starting another, if one's pupil happened to be the Shogun, he might be granted a sort of 'honorary *menkyo*' for appearance's sake. For instance the Yagyū gave the following document to the third Tokugawa Shogun, Iemitsu: 'You have received everything, including the weak points of our style, originated by Kamiizumi Nobutsuna, the secret techniques, and the secrets of preparation of mind and body, all the techniques you have learnt from a young age, and our style covering all the weak points. May the various gods and Buddhas punish you if you reveal it.' Needless to say, the Shogun had not actually been given any great secrets, but Iemitsu was certainly a keen and a dedicated swordsman, and summoned fighters from all over the country for regular tournaments. On receiving the document Iemitsu then gave a promise called a *kishōmon* to the master Yagyū Munenori, promising to the gods not to pass on anything to anyone unauthorized to receive it. This was a formality used when any techniques were passed on to a pupil, either verbally or written. The pupil in receipt of a *menkyo-kaiden* would then customarily express his gratitude in the form of a gift.

Several of these so-called secret documents have survived, but little enlightenment can be gleaned from them nowadays for *kendō* enthusiasts. In essence they were only outlines or summaries of important things passed on only verbally. Even the drawings of fighting positions contained in some are difficult to interpret. They acted in effect as an 'aide-mémoire' to the techniques that had already been learned practically, and of course, in the case of passing on an inheritance, the mere possession of the documents indicated the legality of succession, whatever they actually said. This was to have an important bearing on the bizarre way in which the succession was passed on in the Itto-ryū.

The fight for succession

There can be no greater contrast to the orderly transfer of inheritance within the Yagyū Shinkage-ryū, than the extraordinary affair within the Itto-ryū, the other school of swordsmanship to become tutors to the Tokugawa family. Their *sensei*, and great rival to the Yagyū, was Ono Tadaaki, the contemporary of Yagyū Munenori.

Ono Tadaaki has already been mentioned in a previous chapter in connection with the disciplinary action brought against him when he broke ranks to pursue a challenge during the siege of Ueda castle in 1600. The whole of Ono Tadaaki's career, and indeed that of his master Itto Ittōsai Kagehisa, has this wild aspect to it, a trait which can be made to fit in well with the strange lone figure of Miyamoto Musashi, but not with a man who is *kenjutsu* instructor to the Shogun. Apparently Ono Tadaaki literally never pulled punches with his *bokutō* when practising with Tokugawa Hidetada, leaving the heir to the Shogunate with many painful bruises. It is hardly surprising that once Hidetada succeeded as Shogun he tended to favour the more diplomatic Yagyū Shinkage-ryū to the brusque Itto-ryū.

Much of Ono Tadaaki's attitude stemmed from his *sensei* Itō Ittōsai, who was himself a hard taskmaster. But the major difference between Itō Ittōsai and the other legendary *kengō* such as Tsukahara Bokuden and Miyamoto Musashi is that every other master swordsman sought at some time or another in his career to discover a deep religious, philosophical or moral element in the practice of swordsmanship. Miyamoto Musashi wrote his famous *Gorinshō*, the 'Book of Five Rings'. The Yagyū family produced treatises on swordfighting, seeing the wielding of a sword as being a way of preserving and enhancing life rather than merely destroying it. But Itō Ittōsai was different. He devoted himself totally to

THE TEACHER

swordsmanship as the art of wielding a sword. To him there was no inner meaning, no philosophical link with Zen Buddhism or Confucianism, just the single-minded goal of perfection in the art of fighting with a sword. The cynical would call him an inhuman butcher. Others, perhaps, who see Ittōsai's career in the context of the turbulent Sengoku Period, might call him a realist.

His life is more shrouded in mystery than many of his contemporaries. According to different accounts, he was born either in 1550 or 1560, came from any one of three locations and supposedly lived until his nineties. He exhibited the precocity of youth recorded for every great *kengō*, and received training in the Chūjō-ryū under the direction of Kanemaki Jissai. Kanemaki-*sensei* was the former pupil of Toda Seigen, whose inspired use of a piece of firewood we noted in the previous chapter.

Sasaki Ganryū, defeated by Miyamoto Musashi, had also been Kanemaki Jissai's pupil, so his was a school to be reckoned with.

After a period of time with Jissai, Ittōsai left to found his own school based on the Chūjō-ryū which he called, unsurprisingly, the Ittō-ryū. His skills were very highly regarded, and he had the unusual compliment paid to him, albeit posthumously, by having a book published about him by the grandson of one of his pupils, Kofujita Kageyu. The book, published in 1653 under the title

▼ **Kanemaki Jissai** Kanemaki Jissai was a renowned *sensei* of the Chūjō-ryū in the late sixteenth century. He was a pupil of Toda Seigen, and his own pupils included Itō Ittōsai and Sasaki Ganryū.

THE FIGHT FOR SUCCESSION

Ittōsai Sensei Kemposhō, is a seminal work on swordsmanship and the more practical side of the values later to be known as *bushidō*. Itō Ittōsai is best remembered, however, for the quite extraordinary way in which he chose his successor. In contrast to the solemn passing on of tradition and secrets from Nobutsuna to Yagyū Muneyoshi, or the careful entrusting to a third party of Bokuden's *hitotsu-tachi* secrets, Itō Ittōsai made two of his disciples fight a duel to decide who should inherit. The pupils were a man called Zenki, who had formerly worked as a ferryman, and Tenzen, whom Ittōsai had once defeated in a *bokutō* duel. The fight between Zenki and Tenzen took place early one morning in 1588. As his pupils, armed with real swords, prepared to take up their positions, Ittōsai placed on the ground the official scrolls containing the *menkyo-kaiden* of the school, possession

of which would confirm the new master. The pupils drew, and waited, each so thoroughly aware of the other's techniques, and so keenly sensitive to the other's body language, that for a long period of time they stood like statues. Then Zenki moved, but not to the attack. Instead he dashed over and picked up the scrolls, proclaiming himself as the winner. Tenzen chased after him as Zenki fled with the documents that would be accepted as proof of his succession by every swordsman in Japan. Tenzen

---

▼ **Itō Ittōsai and Ono Tadaaki** This illustration shows the *sensei* Itō Ittōsai passing on to his successor Tenzen (Ono Tadaaki) the secret scrolls that indicated his inheritance of the Ittō-ryū. Tenzen won the right to succeed by fighting a duel with a rival pupil.

THE TEACHER

caught him at the edge of a grove of trees and brought his sword down on to Zenki's shoulder, practically cutting him in two. That was the violent way in which Tenzen, henceforth known as Ono Tadaaki, inherited the Ittō-ryū.

There are many other stories concerning the transfer of power within a *ryū*, from tales of squabbles between sons, to the devising of tests to decide the best swordsman. Tsukahara Bokuden, according to legend, tested his three sons by balancing a piece of wood on top of the door so that it would fall on them when they entered. One son caught the wood in mid-air. Another cut clean through it with his sword in a *hitotsu-tachi* stroke, but the succession went to the son who refused to enter by the door until he had checked to see if there were a piece of wood ready to fall on him! No *sensei* other than Itō Ittōsai specified anything so dramatic as a fight to the death. One, however, got one almost by default, when

his inheritance was finally settled by a duel on a bridge between his natural successor, and one who disputed it.

The dying sensei

During the latter half of the Sengoku Period, in present-day Edosaki in Ibaraki Prefecture, there was a *sensei* called Morooka Ippa. Ippa may have been a pupil of either the Tenshin Shōden Shintō-ryū, or of Bokuden's Shintō-ryū, but whatever his origins, he was a fine swordsman and a devoted *sensei*. But there was one black cloud on Ippa's horizon. He had very delicate health. Ippa was in fact suffering from leprosy, a disease for which contemporary medicine could offer no cure. As his swordfighting skills diminished with the decline in his physical health, so the numbers of his pupils dwindled. Finally he had only three senior pupils left: Negishi Tokaku, Iwama Koguma and Hijiko Doronosuke.

THE DYING SENSEI

The three men pledged their best efforts to attend to their master's troubles, and to preserve his teachings. However, that night, Negishi Tokaku fled, unwilling to restrict his own prowess by service to a dying master. By contrast Koguma and Doronosuke were determined not to abandon their master in his serious illness. Such a course of action was unthinkable to faithful samurai who had received so much from their master's deep kindness. This principle of responding to a lord's 'benevolence' by loyalty, was to become a cornerstone of *bushidō*.

Koguma and Doronosuke went without meals and suffered poverty in order to be able to supply medicines for their master. At one time they even pawned their swords, and sold their clothes for cash. But after three years of rudimentary medical skills and devoted nursing the great master Morooka died, to be followed shortly by one of his two devoted pupils Hijiko Doronosuke. At this stage the other senior pupil, Tokaku, re-enters the story. He had gone to the city of Odawara, where he had made a name for himself as a swordsman, associating himself with another *sensei* called Tenka Musō, a strange character who in addition to being a swordsman was also a *yamabushi*, a member of the mystical Buddhist sect of Shugendō who went on austere mountain pilgrimages. There were many legends about him, such as the performance of magic, or that he was really a *tengu*. Tokaku was supposed to have been initiated into the secret arts by Musō, and had made a scandalous name for himself in Odawara.

Hearing of the *sensei's* death Tokaku proclaimed himself as the heir to the *ryū* by virtue of being the most accomplished swordsman, a claim that scandalized the faithful Koguma. Only a duel between the two of them could settle the inheritance, and hearing that Tokaku had made his temporary base in Edo, he resolved that the decisive contest should be carried out there. It was now 1593, and at this time Edo Castle (now the palace of the Emperor of Japan) was not finished. The Tokugawa, who were to become the ruling Shogunal family, were at the time just one other *daimyō* family, and non-family members could pass quite freely within its moats. In front of the Ōte gate Koguma fixed a noticeboard on which he had written: 'For persons who aspire to the military arts, victory or defeat will alone decide the inheritance bet-

ween master and pupil. Iwama Koguma.' Koguma intended this to be a provocation to Tokaku. If Tokaku heard of this noticeboard he would certainly guess the meaning behind the strange wording, which implied a recognition by Koguma that he accepted the principle that the most skilled swordsman should inherit. Very soon the challenge was taken up, and the site of the contest was to be the bridge in front of the Ōte gate where Koguma had set up his notice. Both parties would have *bokutō* for the fight.

By this time Koguma's physical appearance was dreadful. His enforced poverty had made him thin and wasted, and his clothes were very poor-looking for a young man. By contrast the taller than average Tokaku cut a dashing figure, and judging by his appearance alone the numerous sightseers expected to see a quick victory. He wore a satin *kosode* (robe) and *hakama* (divided skirt-like trousers) of white cloth with black leggings, and wore straw *waraji* on his feet. He carried a very long and unusual *bokutō* of hexagonal cross-section, reinforced with iron here and there, while Koguma had only an ordinary one. Koguma strode on to the Ōte bridge from the west, while the confident Tokaku virtually danced in from the east, swinging his large *bokutō*. The despised Koguma held his weapon in the high position known as *jōdan*. Koguma was a small man, but one capable of a great deal of cleverness, and he was looking for that brief instant when Tokaku might drop his guard. Sensing the moment, he took the opportunity and lowered his *bokutō* slowly to *gedan*, the low posture, which looked deceptively unguarded.

Accounts of what happened during the next few seconds become very confusing, and there are several theories about this unusual contest to explain why it was that without landing one blow on Koguma, the haughty Tokaku found himself falling from the parapet of the bridge into the river. The idea has been suggested that Tokaku tried to land a blow, but that Koguma side-stepped, allowing the momentum of the heavy *bokutō* to disturb Tokaku's own balance as in one of the modern *kata* of *aikidō*, whereupon Koguma pushed him to the side of the bridge, and lifted him below his hips so that Tokaku fell upside-down into the river. That is one theory. There is an alternative, that Koguma was pushed by Tokaku against the railings of the bridge, but suddenly took Tokaku's leg to off-balance him, then pulled him down and over into the river using a throw similar to the

◀ **A swordfight** The *Ehon Taikō-ki* shows us a fierce contest between non-armoured swordsmen and samurai.

THE TEACHER

tomoe-nage throw of *jūdō*, whereby the opponent somersaults over the thrower.

Whatever the theorists say, they agree that he avoided Tokaku's blow, and pushed his opponent over the railings, so there was no longer any doubt as to who should follow Morooka Ippa as *sensei*. Tokaku had behaved recklessly, and to be thrown into the river with his own sword neutralized was a symbolic end for him. Koguma had appreciated his own limitations, and had thought how to turn his opponent's strength and greater skill against him. He had learnt and read much during his master's serious illness, and as well as being the one not to abandon his master, had positively benefited from the experience. From this time the name of Tokaku virtually disappears from history. It is believed that he changed his name and eventually took service with Kuroda Nagamasa, the lord of a province far from the scene of his disgrace.

The rival schools

Duels were occasionally used not to determine the successor to a *ryū*, but to decide the choice of the best school for a *daimyō's* retainers. No school could hope to have a constant and unchallenged monopoly of service. One example is the Taisha-ryū of Kyūshū, founded by Marume Kurandō, whose early career we described above. The reputation of the Taisha-ryū suffered badly from Hideyoshi's defeat of the Shimazu clan in 1587. Among the disillusioned Shimazu men was Tōgō Shigekata, who reasoned that by using the teachings of the Taisha-ryū the Shimazu had been defeated, and he perceived the need to found a new school.

In 1588, in order to display his loyalty to Hideyoshi, Shimazu Yoshihisa went to Kyōto. Shigekata was ordered to be his attendant, and took the opportunity to be taught fencing by the priest Zankitsu of the Jigen-ryū, which emphasized the need for Zen meditation. Soon Shigekatsu returned to Satsuma, eager to prove the worth of the new *ryū*. This finally happened in 1601 when Iehisa followed Yoshihiro as daimyō. Iehisa was the sole Shimazu family member who had favoured the Jigen-ryū and in 1604 Iehisa ordered a *taryū-jiai* contest between the two schools. Shigekatsu was to fight for the Jigen-ryū and the Shimazu family *sensei* Kō Shin-no-jō for the Taisha-ryū. Shin-no-jō was the son of former *sensei* of the Taisha-ryū under whom Shigekatsu had originally

▲ **Negishi Tokaku in the river** Two swordsmen fought each other on a bridge in Edo for the right to succeed their late master Morooka Ippa. The haughty Negishi Tokaku ended up being thrown over the parapet into the river by the victor Iwama Koguma.

studied. It was a deeply emotional occasion for Shigekatsu, but his trouble and hard work bore fruit, and he was victorious. The Jigen-ryū then became the official school to the Shimazu *daimyō*.

The school that fought to survive

The Nen-ryū is the last of the four schools regarded as the classical swordfighting *ryū* of Japan, the others being the Tenshin Shōden Shintō-ryū, the Chūjō-ryū, (which continued as the Ittō-ryū), and the Kage-ryū. It is now called the Maniwa Nen-ryū, the word Maniwa referring to a place in Kōzuke province where it made its base in the late sixteenth century.

The founder of the Maniwa Nen-ryū, Higuchi Matashichirō, was descended from a follower of Kiso Yoshinaka, one of the leading samurai in the Gempei War. The Higuchi family, a country samurai family of modest means, moved to Maniwa in 1500, where they remain to this day. The tradition of the Nen-ryū, however, predated the move to Maniwa, and is commonly traced back to a certain Sōma Yoshimoto, who lived at about the end of the twelfth century, which if true, would make it much older than the Shintō-ryū. According to legend, when Yoshimoto was five years old his father was murdered, and Yoshimoto was taken by his wet-nurse to a place of safety to be brought up as a monk. Yoshimoto swore vengeance for his father, and learned secret methods of sword fighting from a priest of Kamakura. When he was eighteen he returned to his home town and fulfilled his vow of vengeance, and after that he entered the Zen sect. On founding his own temple he changed his name to Nen Oshō, which is the origin of the name Nen-ryū.

One of Nen Oshō's finest pupils was a member of the Higuchi family. However the tradition was not followed continuously within the main line of the family, there being a break of about four generations before the seventeenth-generation Matashichirō in the 1590s. The Shintō-ryū had become the Higuchi family's new tradition, with the Nen-ryū tradition almost completely forgotten. Matashichirō, who ran a *dōjō* in Maniwa, was a skilled swordsman, and wanted to learn the truth about the fundamentals of the Nen-ryū which he could only glean from writings of the family because he thought it had died out. Young Matashichirō was very disappointed at the lack of continuity of what had once been a family tradition.

Then one day a distant relative called Konishi Kyōbei appeared. Kyōbei had had a fairly good technique, learned from the Shintō-ryū, but had never been as good as Matashichirō. The unfortunate Kyōbei had however recently developed an eye disease, and because of this he had been two months without sight. In spite of his handicap Kyōbei could not resist challenging his relative to a fight. Of course Matashichirō accepted, and to his surprise he was defeated by the blind man. They fought again, but the result was the same. Kyōbei had a strange power which Matashichirō had never encountered before. Kyōbei attributed it to an eye doctor whom he had consulted called Tomomatsu Gian, who was also a skilled swordfighter, and had taught him the innovative methods. On further questioning this Gian turned out to be be the seventh-generation master who had received directly the Nen-ryū tradition. Matashichirō's eyes shone.

▲ **The grave of Higuchi Matashichirō** Higuchi Matashichirō was the founder of the Maniwa Nen-ryū, one of the few surviving authentic schools of traditional *bugei*.

THE TEACHER

This was the opportunity to re-establish the family link with the Nen-ryū. He immediately went to be a pupil of Gian, leaving his *dōjō* under the care of his younger brother. He travelled through many provinces on a *musha-shugyō*, carrying the master's medicine chest on his back, training with him as he travelled. In 1590 he returned to the Maniwa *dōjō*. In 1595 he received the *menkyo-kaiden* of the Nen-ryū and in 1598 became the eighth master of the Nen-ryū. This was the origin of the Maniwa Nen-ryū.

The duel on the riverbank

At that time, in the nearby castle town of Takasaki, there was a person called Murakami Tenryū of the Tendō-ryū. He was said to have been born in Kashima and in a mere three years about a hundred pupils had passed through his hands. He was of a proud nature, and a man of the greatest strength and ability, but he had a reckless personality which he had in common with his master Saitō Denkibō, whose untimely death was recounted in a previous chapter. As ill luck would have it, the village

which contained the Maniwa Nen-ryū *dōjō* was not far away. A new *ryū* to rival the Tendō-ryū had been founded, run by a mere local village samurai!

Tenryū sent a written challenge to the Maniwa *dōjō*, but Matashichirō had made it a rule that *taryū-jiai* were banned, and thus he politely refused. For a second time Tenryū issued the written challenge, and received the same reply. Of course the Tenryū side denounced Matashichirō as a coward, and began to ridicule the talents of the Nen-ryū. However the pupils of the Maniwa side managed to keep silent, until they could no longer let the situation lie, and Matashichirō was forced to accept. It was a contest he had to win. A defeat would destroy both his life and the meaning of the Nen-ryū. So he visited the Yamana Hachiman shrine in a nearby village, and vowed to defend the honour of the Maniwa Nen-ryū. There is a stone (the sword vow stone)

▼ **The sword-vow stone** This stone in the Yamana Hachiman shrine commemorates the pledge by Higuchi Matashichirō, founder of the Maniwa Nen-ryū.

THE DUEL ON THE RIVERBANK

commemorating the fulfilment of his vow in the same shrine to this day.

Thus, in March 1600, on the banks of the Karasugawa in Kōzuke Province a duel was fought which risked the future of two schools of martial arts. The fight began at the hour of the dragon (8.00 a.m.). The surface of the water was covered in mist, and the sound of the running water was very clear. An intense and expectant atmosphere hung over the scene. The rivals fought within a bamboo fence, outside which were the pupils from the two schools and also crowds of people from the castle town, samurai, townspeople and farmers from the nearby villages, leaving their work to see the fight. As the moment approached everyone swallowed hard with anticipation, waiting to see the two men, Matashichirō and Tenryū, walk up. Matashichirō had a *bokutō* carved from loquat wood. They were of equal height, and both were imposing figures.

The contest began from the moment when both men entered within the barrier, and it was decided within seconds. Seeing Matashichirō apparently totally relaxed and calm, Tenryū charged forward quickly shouting, 'I have won!', and waved his sword rather than lowering it in a defensive guard position. He rushed in only to have Matashichirō's loquat *bokutō* smashed against the upper half of his face. Tenryū fell on his back with his mouth open, from which clots of blood gurgled forth, and his body fell to the ground. As he tried to get up he dropped his own sword, and received a blow on top of the head from Matashichirō's furious weapon. This one blow decided the future of one of the greatest *sensei* of the Sengoku Period, and also the future of the Maniwa Nen-ryū, which is today one of the few authentic schools of traditional *bugei* (martial arts) left in Japan.

In common with all other schools, the Maniwa Nen-ryū soon had to cope with the new demands made by the years of peace. The initial decline, and the revival during the nineteenth century, will be the theme of the following chapters.

▼ **A fight with *bokutō*** Two Samurai engage each other with *bokutō*. **Note the absence of sword guards. (From the *Ehon Taikō-ki*)**

8.

The Criminal

It is not often recognised how much the popular image of the wandering lone samurai owes to members of the non-samurai classes, or to the criminal element of Old Japan. To some extent the same is also true of the image of the martial arts, which are commonly regarded as samurai arts, the preserve of the aristocratic military class, involving esoteric techniques that were never taught to the lower orders. In fact many of the techniques that nowadays come under the heading of martial arts owed much of their development to the need to provide what one might call 'anti-samurai' arts, as townsmen and farmers, deprived of the right to carry weapons, turned to techniques involving simple weapons and bare hands to defend themselves against any abuse of power by their betters.

Some well-respected writers go even further in their analysis. According to Yamada, in his study of *kenjutsu*, the elevation of swordsmanship to a quasi-religious and aesthetic status did not originate with the samurai class who, despite their great experience in battle, had neither the time nor the inclination to practise fine technique, let alone raise it to an art form. For the battle-hardened warrior swordfighting was a savage and anonymous business of hacking, from which only a genius such as Kamiizumi Nobutsuna could lift himself. To Yamada the greatest prowess in swordsmanship arose instead from people who had been forced to make up a deficiency in physical strength and battle experience by learning to handle the sword in a manner that was technically expert. Practice in this, which could only be conducted away from the battlefield, inevitably led to swordsmanship being seen more as an art than as a series of techniques.

In contrast we have Kōsaka Danjō, the author of the *Kōyō Gunkan*, who died in 1578 and was a samurai general of the Takeda. Kōsaka Danjō maintained that swordsmanship could only be learned on a battlefield. In times of peace, when there was nothing to fight for, a samurai only learnt *kata*, the series of formal exercises. Battlefield fighting was therefore the natural way to train, and the only realistic way. As the *Kōyō Gunkan* was published in twenty editions from 1600 to 1750 his words were undoubtedly influential.

The samurai decline

We will develop this argument more fully in the chapter on *bushidō* which follows, but as the 'Age of War' gave

THE SAMURAI DECLINE

▲ **A makeshift weapon** Several of the so-called 'samurai fighting arts' developed from the need for lower-class persons to defend themselves against the abuse of power by samurai. Here a farmer rushes into action wielding a hoe.

way to the two and a half centuries of the 'Age of Peace', represented by the ascendancy of the Tokugawa family, there is ample evidence that the mainstream martial skills of sword, spear and bow suffered something of a decline among the samurai class, even among the close retainers of the Shogun, with not much replacement visible in the form of an 'art'. Kōsaka Danjō's claim that the battlefield was the only place to learn true martial skills seemed to be coming more true with every peaceful year that passed. In his book *Taiheisaku* Ogyū Sorai (1666–1728) denounced what he saw as the bad behaviour of his class:

'They conduct themselves in the town with their fearful appearance and thrust-out elbows. With their power to punish they suppress people and create

disorder in society . . . They merely study the stories of warfare and the combative method. Or, perhaps they believe that the mere acquisition of their professional skills is the way of the warrior.'

Other writers bemoaned the fact that the bad behaviour to which Sorai referred was all that samurai seemed capable of, that their warrior skills had been totally ignored, handing over the practice of the martial arts to the criminal element among the lower classes. This was a very serious accusation to make, but had some validity in the analogy with the appreciation of aesthetic matters. As the years of peace wore on, traditional samurai accomplishments such as the *Nō* theatre and the tea ceremony declined against the growing and vibrant culture of the new bourgeoisie of the towns. Wealthy merchants commissioned works of art, and the lively *kabuki* theatre began to attract samurai to see their own lifestyle dramatized and often ridiculed. Meanwhile their martial skills were being similarly hijacked by other, and less savoury elements, in society.

In 1650 a law was passed forbidding duelling among idle members of the Shogun's guard, and even more extraordinarily, in 1694 another law was passed enforcing the practice of martial arts by samurai. Part of the reason for this was the increasing poverty in which many samurai found themselves. To live in a town on a fixed stipend, surrounded by numerous pleasures, rising prices, and obviously wealthy townspeople, was not an environment conducive to a single-minded concentration on the samurai ideal, particularly when there seemed to be little use for their traditional skills. Many took part-time jobs. A few, apparently, pawned their swordblades, replacing them with pieces of bamboo to hold the fittings and scabbard together. Another critic of the samurai character, Murata Seifu (1746–1811), wrote that 'only the swords in their belts reminded them that they were samurai . . .' Perhaps it is just as well that Seifu did not examine many swords very closely!

There were exceptions of course, and examples can be found of samurai who maintained their training in order to carry out a revenge killing, or to serve more loyally as *daimyō's* retainers. To these men, who patronized the *ryū*, swordfighting was indeed an 'art'. We shall also see in a later chapter how something of a general revival occurred towards the end of the Tokugawa Period. But some facts speak for themselves, such as the observation

▲ **Streetfighting in Edo Japan!** An illustration from the *Ehon Taikō-ki* showing the use of *jū-jutsu* techniques in a confrontation in a street.

that by 1720 many of the swordsmiths in the city of Kanazawa spent more time making pots and pans than swords. At the same time, the newly pacific samurai frequently found that the skills which they thought had been theirs alone were far more widely spread within society than they had thought possible. Wandering *rōnin* out on the high roads, plying their samurai swords for hire, could as easily prove to be absconding peasants or petty criminals as samurai. On many occasions samurai found themselves up against well-organized gangs of swordsmen every bit as well-trained and well-armed as they were, skilled in the martial arts, and who owed equally firm allegiance to their own variety of *daimyō*.

In theory, at any rate, this was a situation that could not possibly exist, because according to law and estab-

lished precedent members of the samurai class were the only people allowed to carry swords. It was the wearing of swords that defined a samurai, as his privilege and his right. A series of edicts, beginning with Hideyoshi's famous 'Sword Hunt' of 1587, had set this trend in motion, and had theoretically disarmed all but the samurai class. In practice swords, spears, guns and other weapons were readily obtainable and well-used, sometimes by criminals, otherwise by desperate gangs of lower-class citizens upholding their rights and their lives against the abuse of power by samurai.

The most visible 'non-samurai' lived in the big cities of the Edo Period. They called themselves *otokodate* ('chivalrous fellows') who belonged to the *machi-yakko* (town gangs) and walked openly in the streets in defiance of rules forbidding them swords. They also developed the art of combat with other weapons such as the six-foot staff, or *bō*, and the shorter four-foot *jō*, and became accomplished in the art of the *tantō* (dagger) which could be concealed under clothes, and the defensive use of implements such as the *tessen*, the iron war-fan. It is to men like these, rather than samurai, that the development of minor martial weapons owes a great deal.

Police, outcasts and the martial arts

As a general rule it was not samurai of the Shogun's army who had to deal with such men and their weapons, but the *yoriki* and the *dōshin*, the police force of Tokugawa Japan. The *yoriki* were very familiar with their territory, but lived in a social limbo between the townspeople whose lives they controlled, and the samurai of the castle. The latter would have nothing to do with them because of the ancient Shintō fear of pollution from

▼ **The use of chain weapons** A demonstration of the use of weighted chains to catch a sword blade.

people who had connection with death when criminals were executed. In fact the *yoriki* did not actually carry out executions. That was left to the outcast *hinin*, the 'non-humans', but the mere association with such practices, and their own fierce pride, kept the *yoriki* apart.

Serving under the *yoriki* were the *dōshin*, who played the role of the policeman 'on the beat'. They wore tight-fitting trousers rather than *hakama*, and carried only one sword, though they were regarded as being of samurai status. They were instantly recognizable by a distinctive side-arm which was a badge of office and a vital defensive weapon. This was the *jitte*, a steel rod fitted with a handle, and with one or two hooks along the edge of the 'blade'. The purpose of the *jitte* was to catch a sword stroke so that a felon could be taken alive. In addition to the *jitte* the *dōshin* were armed with a range of fierce-looking hooked and barbed spears, which kept the swordsman at bay, pinned him into a corner, or could usefully entangle items of clothing as he tried to escape. Once the man was cornered and disarmed he was rapidly tied up, and there existed a whole specialist area of 'martial arts' techniques for quickly and securely roping suspects.

Much criminal activity in Tokugawa Japan centred around the provision of illicit gambling dens, particularly at hot spring resorts not far from Edo. In earlier days the recuperative qualities of hot springs were privileges known only to the upper reaches of the samurai class, but as the Tokugawa Period wore on the new bourgeoisie of the merchant class, who already knew the value of hot baths, gained access to these pleasures. The provision of gambling dens promised immense profit for those willing to take a risk, and as they were operating in a very shadowy area of legality it is not surprising that controlling gambling became an activity for organized crime. Some gang-leaders employed people known as *shika-oi*, ('deer chasers') whose job it was to entice customers into the gambling dens, which were often operated under the guise of being a wayside inn. The gangs acquired territories in which their law held sway, much the same as the leaders of the Sengoku warbands had developed into *daimyō*. To such men proficiency at the martial arts was as necessary for their survival as it had been for the samurai of the Sengoku Period. Some of these gang leaders acquired such a reputation for swordsmanship and command that they were employed by the civil authorities to teach swordsmanship to samurai.

THE CRIMINAL

Wanderers and criminals

The great swordsmen who arose from this underclass either worked for the existing authority, hiring to them their swords and their skills, or by choice and pressure of circumstances lived outside the law as outlaws. The outstanding example of the former was a man called Ōmaeda Eigorō, born in 1793 in Kōzuke. He was a famous gambler and big in physique. He trained in swordsmanship at the Maniwa Nen-ryū, evidence in itself of the spread of 'samurai values' throughout society. But he was rarely involved in combat, and used to stop fights between gamblers before blows were exchanged. In his biography he is quoted as saying, 'I killed as many people as my age in years. But all the people I killed were bad men. I was not wrong to kill them.'

His father, Kyūgorō, was very fond of *sumō*. He had a huge body which would have made him a *sumō* wrestler had he chosen such a career, and his son Eigorō proved to be over six feet tall and very big. Kyūgorō became a gambler and formed a group, nicknamed the *takenobori*, his territory being the Akagi mountains. So from a young age Eigorō grew up in a gambler's family, and when he was a youth the village people called him the 'fireball' because he was so boisterous. At the age of sixteen he killed his first victim, Kugū no Jōhachi. Jōhachi had opened a gambling place within Eigorō's father's territory in Yamagi village, where many townsmen and farmers came to market every month. It was also near to the Ōmaeda village, where the Ōmaeda collected a lot of money. Jōhachi clearly wanted to break into the Ōmaeda territory.

Eigorō took his father's part, and killed Jōhachi in his gambling den in 1808. Because he could not return to his home he went to the nearby castle town. It was very late at night, and the one shop that was open was a *tofu* shop where he heard people talking about the murder of Jōhachi. Eigorō guessed the police were looking for someone. He realized the danger and went to Kuwata village where he slept among the hay. The following morning he took his *aikuchi* (a small dagger) and cut the hair off his forehead. This would normally be performed during the *gempuku* ceremony of entry into manhood,

▶ **The bad guys!** A scene from the film *Yōjimbō* showing one of the rival gangs heading off to confront the hero.

WANDERERS AND CRIMINALS

THE CRIMINAL

but Eigorō did it for disguise, because he realized they were looking for a youth. He then escaped to Mino Province until the affair died down, and was never arrested for the crime. He seemed to lead a charmed life, helped by his considerable diplomatic skills with the authorities, and no doubt the occasional handsome bribe.

Most reliable accounts of his life say he was impulsive, active and very fond of fighting, and that his sword technique improved with age. He fought about twenty or thirty times without mishap, except for one occasion in Mino when he killed someone and ran away through the snow and developed frostbite, eventually losing two toes. His sword technique was outstanding, as was his general health, and he finally died in bed at the age of 82.

Kunisada Chūji - swordsman on the run

Kunisada Chūji, like Ōmaeda Eigorō, was born in Kōzuke Province. But in contrast to Eigorō, who built a giant sphere of influence through co-operating with the authorities when it suited him, Chūji lived his life resisting power. He was pursued by officials, and because he opposed authority he became the hero of the common people, and something of a Japanese 'Robin Hood'. Chūji did not however cut a very romantic figure, being short, fat and with a full, light complexion. He began his career as a swordsman as a follower of Ōmaeda Eigorō, to whom he is said to have boasted, 'In one day I can raise 400 men, in ten days I can raise 4,000.' He became so important to Eigorō that he was treated as if he were a younger brother. Chūji put himself outside the law when he killed his rival Shimamura Isaburō in 1834. Their rivalry, inevitably, concerned the question of spheres of influence. Both controlled networks of gambling dens within the province, and as each territory grew a collision became increasingly likely. Shimamura Isaburō was twenty years older than Chūji, and clearly resented the growing power of the younger gang leader. The arrangements Chūji made to kill Isaburō smack of military precision, and the coldest, most calculating mind.

The incident that sparked the vendetta occurred in 1834 when a follower of Chūji called Mitsugi no Bunzo misbehaved in a saké shop as Isaburo was passing. He pulled Bunzo out into the street and thrashed him. Bunzo could not forget this incident and told his boss Chūji, who saw an excuse to get Isaburō's territory. So Chūji planned a sudden attack. Usually he would have announced a

challenge to a rival, but decided on a surprise attack because Isaburō was so good a swordsman. Chūji set off for Serata village where Isaburō had opened his gambling den. Isaburō's last moments are vividly brought to life in the story *Yagi-bushi*. Isaburō was drinking *saké* in a restaurant along with his men. For some reason or other the mouth of the *saké* bottle cracked, which his followers thought to be a bad omen. With all the henchmen surrounding Isaburō for safety they left the *saké*-shop after dark and went to the Chōraku-ji, which Kunisada Chūji had already surveyed for a possible ambush. He had observed that there were two doors to the south from which one could escape, while the way to the north was

▼ The swordsman fugitive Kunisada Chūji, who was crucified in 1850, was one of the most notorious criminal swordsmen of the later Edo Period. Here he examines the head of one his victims, as proud as any *daimyō* of the 'Age of War'. A series of novels and plays made him into something of a 'Robin Hood' character. (Private collection)

KUNISADA CHUJI – SWORDSMAN ON THE RUN

across low ground and through a flooded rice field. That was where Chūji caught Isaburō as he approached. His followers surrounded the house and caused a commotion. Bunzo shouted 'Revenge!' The tall Isaburō was wearing a padded *kimono* with big criss-crosses on it, and was instantly indentifiable. It had started to rain and he had a lantern in one hand and in the other hand an umbrella, which made it difficult for him to get hold of his sword in the case of a sudden attack. When he passed a bush Chūji and Bunzo and ten others came out. Isaburō was killed in one second by a rapid *kesa* strike across the chest.

One of Isaburō's followers was hiding under a bridge and witnessed the entire affair. When the *yoriki* arrived on the scene he came out, but Chūji had gone, leaving nothing behind him but Isaburō's body. Chūji then took over Isaburō's sphere of influence, and his territory began to grow widely. But by so cold-bloodedly mur-

dering a rival he had set himself clearly outside the law. It was soon no longer safe for Chūji to stay in Kōzuke Province, so he set off on a journey, not as a warrior on a pilgrimage, but as a fugitive. Travel from one province to another during the Edo Period, however, was rendered very difficult by the existence of toll-barriers at every crossing point. Chūji determined to flee to Shinano Province, where he could hide among its vast mountains, and broke down the barrier at Oto to make his exit from Kōzuke, an act that earned him as much notoriety and popular fame as had the murder. In Shinano he hid in a village near Akazayama, where he rented another temple and opened a gambling-den.

Here he lived a life of great lawlessness. In 1834 he killed a man from the Tamura family, followed by the man's brother six years later. In 1842, he killed a police spy, Mimura Kansuke, sent to gain information about him. There were feuds among his erstwhile followers, until Shinano became too uncomfortable for him to stay, and for a second time he broke down the Oto barrier. But he had already alienated all his support back in Kōzuke, and the *yoriki* arrested him soon after his return. His

---

▼ **The techniques of roping** There was a whole specialized area of 'martial arts' techniques for securely roping a suspect. This illustration is from the *Ehon Taikō-ki.*

punishment, death by crucifixion, was no more than he deserved, and it is surprising that such an unlikely candidate for heroism should have become a romantic figure.

The Yōjimbō

If a wandering non-samurai swordsman had neither the power nor the wealth to command his own 'private army', there was always employment to be had as a *yōjimbō*, or bodyguard. One of the most entertaining of Toshiro Mifune's film roles is as a *yōjimbō* in the film of the same name, where he plays two gangs of criminals off against each other. It is a classic 'lone samurai' role, with many fierce swordfights and a fitting climax with the hero wandering off into the sunset.

Among their other duties the *yōjimbō* guarded against incursions by burglars, and always kept a *bō* (long staff) beside their beds, hence the name. They would take the *bō* if they heard a door being forced, and tackle an intruder using the techniques of *bōjutsu* rather than

▲ **An ambush** A samurai is cut down from behind by a sword stroke, while his companion is held by a *jū-jutsu* hold.

▶ *Yōjimbō* **on guard** A frame from *Lone Wolf* showing *yōjimbō* guarding a house. (Lone Wolf and Cub © 1989 First Publishing Inc. and Global Communications Corp.)

swordfighting. In common with the official policy of the *dōshin*, and in contrast to the popular image from the movies, to cut a man down in cold blood was not usually acceptable, so the oak *bō* was one way in which he could be restrained. It was in fact a very strong weapon. A swordstroke could be blocked, and a poorly tempered blade shattered if hit correctly, so the odds were not all on the side of the swordsman.

Some merchants in the cities used their own *yōjimbō* to give them protection against the *hatamoto-yakko*, the samurai gangs recruited from idle retainers in the cities who oppressed the citizens. They also hired *yōjimbō* to protect their palanquin carriers. During the seventeenth

THE YOJIMBO

century disorder and crime were so serious in Edo that in 1686 new regulations were introduced to prevent arson and burglary, and in one swoop more than 200 *machi-yakko* men were rounded up and gaoled. The top eleven were executed including the notorious Token Gombei and various other *rōnin*.

Towards the end of the Edo Period, as we noted above, gambling became big business, and to keep others out of their territories the big bosses employed *yōjimbō*.

Yōjimbō at this later date were sometimes second or third sons of samurai who had some experience of learning *kenjutsu* while travelling around in the countryside, so their swordfighting was usually very good. The most famous *yōjimbō* was Hirate Miki, *yōjimbō* to Sasagawa no Shigezo. According to one story he had tried to kill the great *sensei* Chiba Shūsaku and was defeated. He then asked to become his pupil and was forgiven. He was a very skilful pupil, but because he suffered from tuber-

THE CRIMINAL

culosis he became depressed, lost all ambition, and drank heavily. His behaviour became so outrageous that he was finally kicked out by Shūsaku. At that time the Chiba *dōjō* had about 3,600 pupils, so the anecdote may be just fanciful. Because he had no chance of serving a samurai family, and thought he had little life left, he decided to become a *yōjimbō* of a gambler, and went to Choshi, a prosperous fishing port at the mouth of the Tonegawa with its huge flat riverbed. Around Choshi two leaders had their spheres of influence. Their names were Iioka no Sukegorō and Sasagawa no Shigezō. Neither were samurai, and their surnames merely refer to their localities, as the possessive adjective *'no'* indicates. Sukegorō was based in the present-day town of Iioka, and Shigezō held authority in Tosho by the Sasagawa.

During the early 1840s their territories grew rapidly and eventually the two spheres of influence reached their limits. Both men were of equal standing. Sasagawa no Shigezō acted first, and like his contemporary Kunisada Chūji, hatched a plot to murder Iioka no Sukegorō. However, Sukegorō got to hear of the plot and sought to pre-empt it by destroying his rival on a grand and dramatic scale, in a night raid on the Sasagawa head-quarters on the south bank of the Tonegawa in the ninth month of 1844. The result was a frenzied mass-swordfight by moonlight, which by all accounts was a ferocious affair, with all the hallmarks of a medieval battle. Hirate Miki, the *yōjimbō* to the Sasagawa family, was the great fallen hero, the lone warrior *par excellence*, who 'made the blood flow at the Tonegawa dry riverbed'. He made a dramatic fight to the death. As the samurai blades flashed in the moonlight he was severely wounded, escaped and then died. There are various theories that he was wounded in twenty places on his body and died in a nearby bamboo grove.

The spray of blood on Kojinyama

A *yōjimbō* played his part in another gang battle of the later Edo Period. The incident, known as the *'Kojinyama no chi kemuri'* or 'The spray of blood on Kojinyama', has come down to us as a great quarrel, but the reality is that there was no reason for a direct duel between the protagonists, Kira no Nikichi and Anō Toku. It developed however into a classic encounter of the time, the Japanese equivalent of the gunfight at the O.K. Corral, and savage proof of the martial art skills of the criminal classes,

although it is hardly known outside Japan. It was also probably the last such fight to take place, happening as it did while Japan was becoming engulfed in the battles of the Meiji Restoration.

Kira no Nikichi was a *yūkyō*, a name often used for a gangster. One day his close associate Kambe no Naga-kichi came to him to ask a favour. Nikichi and Nagakichi 'shared a saké cup', a relationship that was an excep-tionally close friendship, and the Kojinyama affair began when this Nagakichi asked him to join him in killing a certain Anō Toku. Hearing this even Nikichi was appalled. Anō Toku was an *otōtobun*, a friend treated as a younger brother, and it was hearsay that he had great influence with the local 'big boss' of Ise. Nikichi himself served Shimizu no Jirochō, a remarkable character who was known as the 'First Boss of the Tokaidō Area', who had five hundred henchmen under him. One of his most remarkable feats had been to get parole to compensate for the injuries he suffered when the gaol he was in collapsed in an earthquake! Always popular with his men, he eventually died peacefully at the age of seventy-four.

Nagakichi explained why he wanted Anō Toku dead. He and Anō Toku had been followers of Oiwake no Yūzō, and following the death of their master, his sphere of influence was divided among the two of them, and gradually they asserted their independence from the family. Within Nagakichi's sphere of influence was Hiroseno in Suzuka, which was part of Ise province, and here were Kasatoyama and Kojinyama. Both mountains were more like hills, but on Kasatoyama Prince Yamato was enshrined, and every year there was a great festival. There was also one at Kojinyama Kannon-ji and many people came, including gamblers, a rich source of profit.

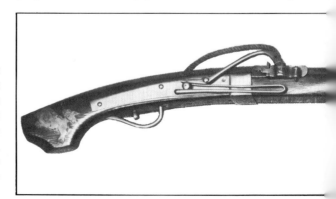

THE SPRAY OF BLOOD ON KOJINYAMA

One year there was a brawl, and Nagakichi killed a merchant by mistake, for which he was sent into temporary exile. He asked a colleague to look after things, but the man was killed by Anō Toku, hence the enmity and the fierce desire for revenge, as ardent as any samurai vendetta.

To further persuade Nikichi to fight, other 'sidekicks' of Shimizu no Jirochō supported Nagakichi's viewpoint, and heaped calumny on Anō Toku. They saw the opportunity of a chance to settle a few old scores, with a noble ideal of vengeance giving it all a spurious justification. Kira no Nikichi also had personal ambitions. If he killed Anō Toku the Shimizu territory would extend into Ise, and he would have a hand in it. Thus a samurai-style vendetta provided a respectable veneer for a gangland feud over territory. So in April 1866, early in the morning, the Kira family group, plus a number of Shimizu swordsmen, about twenty people in all, set off along the river in two fishing boats with all their weapons and food. Anō Toku soon discovered the plot and sent messengers with notice to summon help, including *rōnin*, who met at Kojinyama and set up camp. Here they prepared for a showdown.

◄ Shimizu no Jirochō Jirochō of Shimizu, shown here in a late nineteenth-century engraving, was a powerful gang leader on the Pacific coast, who became known as the 'First Boss of the Tōkai'. One of his claims to fame was to have obtained parole in recompense for the injuries he suffered when the jail in which he was imprisoned was destroyed by an earthquake! (Leyden archive)

▼ An arquebus A gun similar to this was used at the fight on Kojinyama.

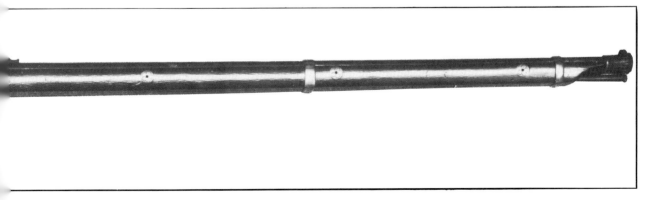

THE CRIMINAL

By now the local *yoriki* had got to hear of the affair and tried desperately to mediate in the dispute, but without success. They finally withdrew, and made ready to return for the bodies. Just after midday a huge fight began, as Kira no Nikichi and the Jirochō henchmen, though heavily outnumbered, attacked the headquarters of Anō Toku in the temple on Kojinyama. The unusual thing about this 'showdown' was that it began as a gun battle reminiscent of the Wild West! Nikichi fought with the *yōjimbō* of Anō Toku, who was called Hakui Moronosuke. First Nikichi tried to fire a matchlock gun at him as he cut down at him, but the gun did not fire. Instead he tried to draw his sword in an *i-ai* stroke, but while doing so was hit by a bullet and dropped his sword. He attempted to pick it up in his left hand but staggered. His comrades saw he was

▼ **Kojinyama is sprayed with blood** This dilapidated little temple building witnessed the Japanese equivalent of the *Gunfight at the O.K. Corral*, when two gangs of rivals attacked each other with swords and guns in 1866.

in danger and rushed to his side. One threw a spear at Moronosuke which wounded him. He stumbled, and seeing him fall another person called Kubi no Saijirō ran up and killed Moronosuke with a quick swordstroke. Anō Toku's faction became distressed because their *yōjimbō* had been killed and started to withdraw, acknowledging their rivals' victory. But Nikichi did not have long to enjoy his triumph, and died shortly afterwards from loss of blood. He was twenty-eight years old.

Thus ended a strange and little known episode in Japanese history, but by this time Japan was on the brink of civil war, and such combats were to be swallowed up in the upheaval of the Meiji Restoration, when martial arts skills were to be needed by all classes, samurai, commoners and criminals alike. Nevertheless the 'Spray of blood on Kojinyama' serves as a reminder that wandering lone warriors and their fighting skills were by no means confined to the samurai classes, and that the Edo Period, for all the absence of war, was by no means a time of peace for everyone.

9.

Bushidō - Spirit of the Samurai

We have noted on several occasions in earlier chapters the influence of the underlying values of the samurai class on their behaviour in battle and their general practice of the martial arts. During the Tokugawa Period these ideas became formulated into the code of conduct known as *bushidō*, the 'Way of the Warrior', a corpus of belief and custom that only began to be formalized once wars had ceased.

This situation of peace was the single most important factor that characterized the time that followed the Sengoku Period. Apart from the brief, but none the less fierce, Shimabara Rebellion in 1638, the only sight of armed men which the Japanese people were to see for two hundred and fifty years were the constant processions along the roads of the *daimyō*, armed to the teeth, but with no purpose beyond that of making their orderly progress to or from Edo to pay their respects to the Shogun. This is the background which must be recognized when studying the topic of *bushidō*, the code of honour and of conduct of the samurai class. In this chapter and the one that follows I intend to examine the nature of *bushidō*, to see in particular how it applied to the samurai as a lone warrior, and what influence it had on the martial arts.

As the study of *bushidō* is the study of the values of the samurai class, our best guide to how they thought and felt about themselves lies in the vast amount of literature produced by and for the samurai class during the Tokugawa Period. In the same way that the *Heike Monogatari* and the *Taiheiki* enshrine the values of an earlier generation of samurai, so do these works express very deep feelings about the Tokugawa samurais' relationships with the rest of society, and with his own peers.

Bushidō has often been mocked as an artificial code of conduct dreamed up by 'armchair samurai' (or 'straw-mat samurai' to keep the metaphor in context!) at least a century removed from actual fighting, to whom the niceties of behaviour could flourish unhampered by any need actually to win battles by applying them. I hope to show that this view is totally unrealistic, and that far from being an archaic, fanciful notion, *bushidō* was a dynamic concept which had real value to the samurai of the age, and arose out of very practical considerations.

There are several reasons why this cynical attitude towards *bushidō* has developed. The first is, quite simply, that the majority of the seminal works on the

BUSHIDO – SPIRIT OF THE SAMURAI

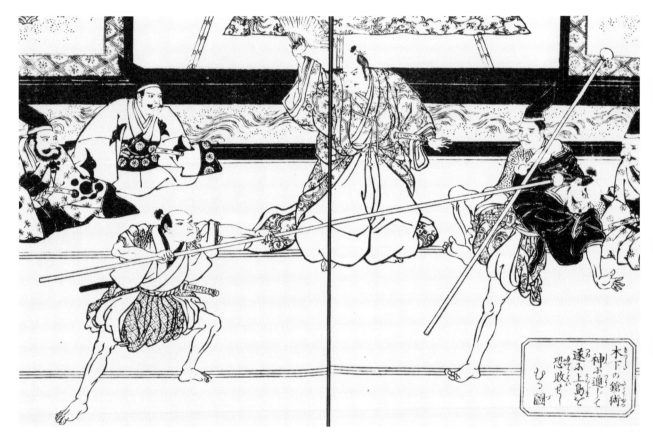

▲ **A spear contest** An illustration from the *Ehon Taikō-ki* depicting a contest using *tampo-yari*, wooden practice spears.

subject, such as the monumental *Kōyō Gunkan*, have never been completely translated into English. (There are valuable exceptions which l list in the bibliography at the end of this book, such as the classic *Hagakure*, and Victor Harris's inspired translation of Miyamoto Musashi's *Gorinshō*, the 'Book of Five Rings'). Second, most views of *bushidō* in the West have been greatly coloured by a book by Inazu Nitobe entitled *Bushidō the Soul of Japan*, which was the first exposition of the concept in the English language. The work is very much a product of its age. It has an extremely optimistic and romantic outlook, which was to turn very sour with the outbreak of the Second World War. The third point, which is to a large extent related to the other two, is that there has been a failure to appreciate the dynamic nature of *bushidō*. Its values changed considerably through the two centuries and a half of Tokugawa rule. This is very much reflected in the literature, and relates very closely to the changing conditions of the military class.

It is convenient, therefore, to divide the development of *bushidō* ideas into four stages. The first stage is the first fifty or so years of the Tokugawa rule, during which the structures erected by the Shoguns was completed, but there was no certainty that wars had actually ceased. The second stage is the last half of the seventeenth century, the real beginning of the age of peace, and a time when the lower classes, particularly the merchants, began to prosper at the expense of the samurai. This was followed by the eighteenth century, when the samurai class was seeking a role for itself as the influences of the preceding century made themselves increasingly felt. As we shall see in a later chapter, the fourth stage, the nineteenth century, presented new challenges to the samurai class in the form of renewed violence and external threat from

BUSHIDO IN EARLY TOKUGAWA JAPAN

overseas, and notions of *bushido* were submerged under the practical need to put into practice these earlier ideals, and awaken the spirit of a past age.

Bushidō in early Tokugawa Japan

The two victories won by Tokugawa Ieyasu, the Battle of Sekigahara in 1600 and the successful completion of the siege of Ōsaka castle in 1615, placed the Tokugawa family in a position that proved to be one of unassailable dominance. But this was a situation to be confirmed only by time, and as the Tokugawa *bakufu* began to construct the political and social system that was to guarantee this dominance, it was by no means clear that wars had actually ceased. Any samurai who counted on a long period of peace would have been an incredibly unrealistic optimist, if the previous century had been anything to go by. Indeed, the Shimabara Rebellion of 1638 showed very clearly that wars had not ceased, and the fact that a motley army of peasants in a dilapidated castle could hold out for so long against a supposedly well-trained *bakufu* army was a portent of a samurai decline. The values which dominated samurai thought at this time were therefore essentially an extension of the values inherited from the previous 'Age of War', so it is worth spending some little time examining what these values were.

The main sources for *bushido*-like values during the Sengoku Period are the *kakun* or house laws of the *sengoku-daimyō*. Several have survived, and all usually make some comment such as 'Study the martial and the literary arts (*bu* and *bun*). Neither must be neglected', or, 'The martial arts and the military arts are like two wheels of a carriage.' There are also some very valuable individual comments, of which the most down to earth is the *kengō* Tsukahara Bokuden's classic comment that

▼ **The sword manual of Yamamoto Kansuke** This illustration is of two pages from a manual on swordsmanship attributed to the general of the Takeda clan Yamamoto Kansuke, to whom swordfighting was a practical skill for use in battle.

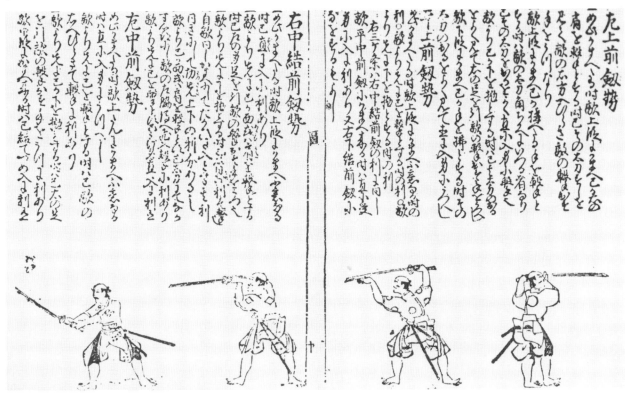

'A samurai who does not know the way of the warrior is like a cat that does not know the way of ratting.' Bokuden also left behind a number of poems, of which the meaning is far less clear. The most celebrated example is his last poem, which reads:

'Let your heart be devoted to study,
But when technique goes awry
Then must the heart lead
Ahead of technique's foolishness.'

Probably the most straightforward statement about samurai values comes from the brush of Torii Mototada (1539–1600). The Torii family were hereditary vassals of the Tokugawa, and in 1600 Torii Mototada was charged with the defence of the castle of Fushimi, to the south of Kyōto. Because of Fushimi's vital strategic location it was likely to prove the first target for Ishida Mitsunari and his allies in the campaign that ultimately was to lead to the decisive Battle of Sekigahara. As part of his diversionary strategy Tokugawa Ieyasu was planning to move his armies to the east to face the threat from the Uesugi, leaving Fushimi perilously isolated, and he confided in Mototada his fears that the Fushimi garrison would be overwhelmed. He intended, he told Mototada, to give him more troops for the defence. But Mototada refused, saying that the castle would fall even if its garrison were increased tenfold, and that his lord would be better served by keeping the other soldiers for the battle that was to come. The duty of the defenders of Fushimi was to hold out for as long as humanly possible against Ishida's attacks until Ieyasu had quelled the rebellion in the east, and had time to return to fight Ishida in the west.

The fight for Fushimi proved every bit as savage and desperate as Torii Mototada and his master had expected, and Mototada was cut down and committed suicide only when the last handful of defenders was overcome, the perfect example of the lone samurai dying a heroic death for his master.

A few days before Ishida's attack began Torii Mototada had written a last letter to his son, which expresses better than any other document of the age the essential values of loyalty to one's lord which lay at the core of bushidō:

'. . . I am resolved to make a stand inside the castle, and to die . . . It would not be difficult to break through the enemy and escape . . . But that is not the true meaning of being a warrior. Instead I shall hold out against the strength of the whole country, without even one hundredth part of the men who would be needed to do so, and I shall defend it and die a glorious death . . . Thus I will have taken an initiative that will strengthen the resolve of Ieyasu's other retainers . . . It is not the Way of the Warrior to be shamed and avoid death . . . to sacrifice one's life for one's master is an unchanging principle.'

He goes on to remind his son of their family and its relationship with the Tokugawa, referring to the 'benevolence' of their lord and the 'blessings' they had received at his hands, and ends with a plea for his son to recognize that the foundation of a samurai's duty is makoto, or 'sincerity'. Makoto is an expression which we will come across time and again in writings on bushidō. It is often used as the ultimate justification for an otherwise apparently wasteful act of self-sacrifice by a defeated samurai who is surrounded by enormous odds, and goes willingly to his extinction because of his makoto. The sincerity of his intentions mingles with the purity of his mission, which requires from him an unflinching devotion to a seemingly hopeless cause.

In the story of Torii Mototada and his makoto we have an expression of bushidō which owes nothing to any sterile formulation dreamt up by a scholar. It is direct, it is uncomplicated, and comes from profound simplicity. In the expressions it uses it also provides several clues for following the development of bushidō as the years of war give way to an uneasy peace. In this context it is instructive to compare the last letter of Torii Mototada with a book written only two decades later by another of Ieyasu's retainers, Okubo Tadataka. Mikawa Monogatari was written in 1622, and attributes Tokugawa Ieyasu's triumph to the close spiritual cohesion he achieved between lord and followers. The word 'benevolence', which Torii Mototada saw as the gift he had received from his lord, is used by Okubo in exactly the same context. The master gives benevolence, the followers respond by loyal and faithful service. Mikawa Monogatari was written during a time when the Okubo were somewhat out of favour with the Shogun, so there is a sense of 'rallying the troops' about it. He is frequently reminding his retainers of the long debt they owed to the Tokugawa, and recommends that they look far beyond their immediate difficulties.

THE COMING OF PEACE

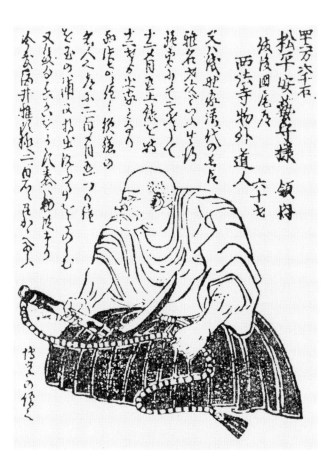

▲ **The kusari-gama** This was a sickle to which was attached a long chain with a weight on the end. It was a formidable weapon in the hands of an expert, making even top-class swordsmen hesitate before attacking.

Similar sentiments are echoed in the other major work of the period, the *Kōyō Gunkan*, which was one of the first written works actually to employ the term *bushidō*. Like *Mikawa Monogatari*, which it predates by half a century, the warrior's code is best expressed in terms of the relationship between master and follower. The first eighteen chapters of *Kōyō Gunkan* were probably written by Kōsaka Danjō, one of the 'Twenty-Four Generals' of the Takeda family, sometime between 1575 and his death in 1578, and the book was completed by his nephew and others. These were tragic times for the Takeda. The great Shingen had died in 1573, while 1575 had seen the cataclysm of the Battle of Nagashino, and the decline and impending destruction of the family. The melancholy gloom of this experience pervades the whole of the work.

Kōsaka derives his image of the ideal warlord from his beloved Shingen, and from the contrast seen in his heir Katsuyori, whose ways led to the clan's downfall. A good leader won battles. A bad leader lost them. But the crucial point is that of the relationship formed between the lord and his followers, exemplified best by the willingness of Shingen's old retainers to serve his son Katsuyori both on and off the battlefield. It was the sincerity to their calling, their *makoto*, that led the old generals of the Takeda to charge the guns at Nagashino. This is *bushidō* at its simple best. It is interesting that Kōsaka also praises the notion of the individual warrior, because the dependence that the samurai has on his lord's benevolence must never become one of over-reliance. The loyalty from a samurai to his lord was loyalty given by a unique individual: 'He makes an effort when preparing himself for action, according to the limits of his capabilities, and in battle he adapts himself to every circumstance in building for himself a reputation for military prowess.' As to the other virtues required by *bushidō*, both Kōsaka and Okubo spoke out forcefully against ostentation in a warrior. 'Maintain this attitude', wrote Okubo, 'even after death from hunger,' a strange foretaste of the famous first sentence in the later *bushidō* classic *Hagakure*, which begins, 'The Way of the Samurai is found in death.' Miyamoto Musashi, too, despised ostentation. In the *Gorinsho* he explains that the swordsman must have total commitment in his striving for excellence and perfection. If this is the warrior's attitude, then there will be no room for ostentation, and the only limit to achieving this perfection will be death, the ultimate proof of service. Yet all insisted that a warrior's life should not be wasted by being thrown away in a street brawl. Such an ignominious end was not in accordance with the Way of the Warrior.

The coming of peace

From 1650 to 1700 Japan experienced a new political stability, and with it an increase in production and urbanization. The samurai class, as the administrators of this new order, had therefore to appreciate the increasingly complex society which they were required to

BUSHIDO — SPIRIT OF THE SAMURAI

govern. A growing merchant and artisan class, with its new wealth, was very visible to the samurai overlords, and the need to understand their relationship with the lower orders coloured the development of *bushidō*. Whereas the balance between loyalty and benevolence sufficed for the active samurai of the early seventeenth century, the writers of the 1650s had to think beyond the battlefield. If the relationship between lord and follower had its deepest expression in a willingness to die for one's lord's benevolence, how could it be expressed when there was nothing to die for? This was one of the questions tackled by Kumazawa Banzan (1619–91), a serving warrior and an accomplished man of letters. He was a samurai in the service of the Ikeda family, who were the *daimyō* of Okayama. As a young samurai he had taken his profession seriously, and practised the martial arts as assiduously as any master swordsman. His spartan regime included eating no rice, and abstaining from sexual relationships. He accompanied the Ikeda on their *sankin kōtai* duties to Edo, when the

daimyō paid his respects to the Shogun, and amused his colleagues by his practice of keeping fit during the boring tours of guard duty by running along the roofs of Edo castle.

Banzan's writings concentrated very much on the background of peace that he saw as having a debilitating effect on the samurai class. The destruction of Ming China by the Manchus alarmed him, and he saw that such a threat might well come the way of Japan if the country did not maintain its defence and military needs. He was particularly critical of the use of the rice stipend as payment for the retained samurai. He urged the quite revolutionary idea that samurai should revert to their former status as farmers, thus both saving rice and producing more that could be stockpiled in case of foreign invasion. 'Ever since the samurai and the farmers have

▼ **Shūriken** Itto Ogami shows one way of dealing with *shūriken*! (Lone Wolf and Cub © 1989 First Publishing Inc. and Global Communications Corp)

CONFUCIUS AND THE SWORDSMEN

▲ **A swordfight** A scene from the film *Sanjurō* showing the lone samurai (Toshiro Mifune) taking on several opponents at once.

become separate classes,' he wrote, 'the samurai have become sickly and their hands and feet have grown weak.'

Confucius and the swordsmen

The writings of Yamaga Sokō (1622–85) concentrate far more on the military aspects of the samurai. He was an early advocate of the need to study western warfare and equipment, a need that was only recognized at a national level two centuries later. Above all, like Kumazawa Banzan, he was profoundly concerned with the inactivity of the samurai class, and a need to find a new role to replace the now unnecessary one of fighting battles.

Yamaga Sokō saw this new role quite simply. The samurai had to serve as a model for society, a view that was very much in line with the current trends towards the ideals of Confucianism, which valued an ordered society where everyone knew his place. Confucianism, along with Zen Buddhism, was one of the philosophical systems which were to influence the notions of *bushidō*, and with it turn swordfighting from an emphasis on technique (*jutsu*) to a 'Way' (*dō*). The *Analects of Confucius* was high on the reading list for any educated warrior, even during the Sengoku Period. In Confucian eyes good government was based on virtue and example rather than on sheer military might. It laid great emphasis on the relationships between people involved in government, and we see Confucian ideals expressed in the use by Kōsaka and Okubo of the terms 'benevolence' and

▲ **Hokusai on archery** A page from Hokusai's sketchbook depicting the positions to be adopted when practising archery. They are very similar to modern *kyūdō*.

approach was to stress the ethical meaning of *kenjutsu*, linking prowess in swordsmanship with the warrior's need to serve his master. Here Confucianism met that other great philosophical influence on *kenjutsu*, the self-denying Buddhism of the Zen sect. Zen Buddhism related swordsmanship directly to the Buddhist goal of attaining enlightenment, and moving towards the achievement of selflessness. By the blending of self and weapon through action the swordsman moved towards the goal of complete emptiness which was the aim of all Zen practices. Much, perhaps too much, has been made of the links between Zen and swordsmanship. In fact swords-manship was the possession of no one philosophical system, and to Confucianism and Zen can be added the influence of the ancient Chinese classics, all of which came together to give the 'Way of the Sword', and with it the 'Way of the Warrior'.

The latter half of the seventeenth century also saw the appearance of two classics of writing about swordsman-ship. The first was the *Fūdochi Shinmyōroku* of the Zen priest Takuan, who taught Zen meditation to Yagyū Munenori. It is a very difficult text to understand, having as its essence the concept of *fūdochi* (permanent wisdom). It means that the working mind, though always changing, is always attached to nothingness, and there-fore to the eternal universe. In contrast is the more down to earth and practical *Ittōsai Sensei Kemposhō*, written in 1653 by Kofujita Toshisada, which is a record of his grandfather's talk on the *kengō* Itō Ittōsai. In common with the philosophy of the *Ittō-ryū*, and in stark contrast to the other writings on *bushidō*, the work is a practical discussion of combat techniques and the application of them to different situations and different opponents. It was a work that the passage of time had of course rendered totally unnecessary. Far from being a necessary skill for daily life, swordsmanship had even ceased to be a means of identifying one social class from another, because all classes now carried swords with impunity. Only a striving for a deep spiritual meaning, which the samurai could then teach to the lower classes, could save *bushidō*.

The reaction to bushidō

The need for a deeper meaning to *bushidō*, and with it a deeper meaning to the life of the peacetime samurai, was the most important challenge facing theorists of the

'loyalty'. The most important ethical demands made by Confucianism were *kō* (filial piety) and *chū* (loyalty), both of which were fundamental to the emerging ideals of *bushidō*. Yamaga Sokō saw the other classes per-forming their functions as farmers, merchants or crafts-men. So should the samurai perform his in the way of serving his lord with exemplary devotion, and with no thought of personal gain. He stressed the traditional samurai values of austerity, self-discipline and readiness to face death. Yet Sokō was wise enough to recognize the difficulty of applying these ideals to the days of peace.

The martial arts too were influenced by Confucian thought. In applying Confucianism to swordsmanship the

THE REACTION TO BUSHIDO

▲ **Jū-Jutsu against an opponent** An illustration from an old manual of *jū-jutsu*, showing two ways of immobilizing an attacker.

eighteenth century, which produced several writers who were very critical of the developing notions of *bushidō*. We noted earlier how Ogyū Sorai (1666–1728) complained about the bad behaviour of the samurai class, and linked this to what he saw as their superficial study of the stories of warfare and combative method. He even went further, and denounced *bushidō* as, 'a bad tradition since the days of the Sengoku Period'. *Bushidō*, as he saw it, was appropriate only for the Age of War, and he criticized the *Kōyō Gunkan* for its historical inaccuracies. To Sorai the true and valuable warrior customs were to be found in the Gempei Wars. These should be the model, not the selfish, land-grabbing *daimyō* of the Sengoku, who attempted to dress up their rapaciousness in a cloak of respectability called *bushidō*. The true benevolence that the samurai class should be seeking was of benevolence towards the lower classes, setting them an example: 'Samurai should . . . maintain to some degree their skills in the martial arts in order to be courageous in action, and to refrain from any excess of personal covetousness. Above all they should be able to guide the warriors in their cultivation for governing the nation.'

Similar notions were also expressed by another Confucian scholar, Yuasa Jōzan (1708–81), who discussed *bushidō* in his work *Jōzan Kidan*, a book which contains many fascinating anecdotes about martial accomplishments. Jōzan does not in fact use the word *bushidō* in his book, largely because, like Sorai, he preferred the warrior ethos of the Gempei War.

The early 1700s also began to see the emergence of the use of *dō* (the way) in describing a training for martial arts that involved the human qualities as well as mere technical skills. As early as 1651 Yamaga Sokō had used the word *dō* in this context, urging his pupils to strive for 'The Way', and one at least of Yamaga Sokō's pupils took heed. This was Ōishi Yoshio, who as leader of the 'Forty-Seven Rōnin' performed the most celebrated act of samurai fidelity in Japanese history. Their action has been much described and discussed, and it will suffice

BUSHIDO – SPIRIT OF THE SAMURAI

here to consider one or two features arising from this classic tale of revenge. The first point to note is the important one that the gallant Forty-Seven's revenge was conducted in such a manner as to put themselves outside the law. As the author explains in the chapter on revenge in *Samurai Warlords*, there were very precise procedural rules for conducting a legal vendetta. The loyal retainers of Ako did not follow them. Their vendetta was carried out in secret, with not even a formal notification to the local magistrates. A further condemnation came from Yamamoto Tsunetomo, author of *Hagakure*, who praised the act of revenge on the grounds that it was to be expected from any samurai at any time, but expressed surprise that it took so long for them to act. To Yamamoto, knowledge should always be accompanied by action, a trend in Confucian thought associated with the writings of Wang Yang Ming that was to lead

ultimately to the dramatic 'actions' of the young revolutionaries of the Meiji Restoration.

In conclusion, *bushidō* during the Edo Period was a dynamic and developing concept, which had as its origins the nature of the relationship that existed between a samurai and the lord he served. In return for the lord's benevolence the samurai rendered loyalty and obedience, behaving at all times in a way consistent with his status in society. The guiding principle was *makoto*, or sincerity, a fidelity to the Way of the Warrior that could often lead to his willing destruction.

▼ **The Forty-Seven Rōnin** The story of the Forty-Seven Rōnin is the classic account of the practical application of the ideas of *bushidō*, but even this epic was not without its critics. One writer went so far as to condemn the loyal retainers for the length of time they took before acting.

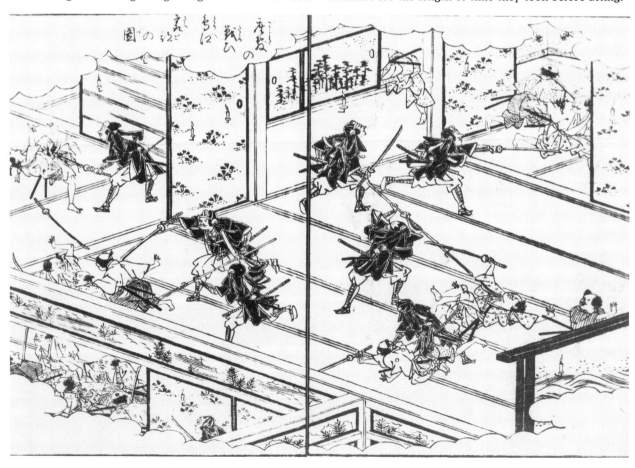

10.

The Martial Arts during the Edo Period

Writers on *bushidō* such as Yamaga Sokō were preoccupied with the need for the samurai class to find a role for itself. As we have seen, a common conclusion they came to was that their most important role was to set an example of moral behaviour to the lower classes. In this chapter I intend to take a brief look at one particular way in which a member of the samurai class was able to set such an example, while at the same time making a statement about himself as a member of an exclusive military élite. This was through the practice of *bugei*, the martial arts.

As with *bushidō*, we see a continually changing shift of emphasis, and a similar dynamic nature. In fact, during the early Edo Period the whole tenor of *bugei* was one of learning and practising actual fighting techniques that would be applied in battle once wars came again. There is a parallel with *bushidō*'s second period as well, when the samurai were forced to work out a new role for themselves. Here *bugei* became a badge of the samurai class, a corpus of skills that distinguished a samurai from the low orders. Later on *bugei* spread to other classes, and was studied more and more for its own sake.

Bugei and Budō

It is important to begin with a clarification about the use of the words 'martial arts'. The two words *bugei* and *budō* are both commonly translated as 'martial arts', but there is an important distinction between them. *Bugei* is an ancient word which appears in very early chronicles, and refers to actual combat, or practice that is designed specifically for such a situation. The only concession made in such practice is the substitute of dummy swords or spears for real weapons, and the widespread use of *kata* rather than actual combat for practising. *Kata*, being a series of standard forms, trained the fighter to react effectively and quickly to a vast range of likely attacks. The coming of peace allowed *bugei* to be practised for their own sake rather than as a training exercise, with much more emphasis on *kata* for safety, but the reality of the situation they represented was always borne in mind. The various arts of *bugei* bear the suffix *-jutsu* (technique) as in *kenjutsu*, *yari-jutsu*, etc., hence the other word for *bugei*, *bujutsu*.

Budō, which uses the character *-dō* (way), such as *kendō*, *aikidō*, etc., are the modern forms far removed

THE MARTIAL ARTS DURING THE EDO PERIOD

▲ **Jū-jutsu** A detail from an illustration in the *Ehon Taikō-ki* showing the use of a shoulder-throw against an armed man. This can be compared to the *seoi-nage* throw of modern *jūdō*.

from the actual combat situation, substituting friendly combat for life or death duels. There are however some instances in the literature of the Edo Period when *-dō* is used instead of *-jutsu*, implying that the ancient *bugei* skills are studied for their own sake rather than for combat practice. The modern usage of *budō* is different. Modern *budō* forms may have a competitive or a sporting context, but this is by no means universal. There is often a reduced emphasis on *kata*, the safety element being

taken care of by modifying either the weapons used, the protection worn, or the moves carried out. Thus the historic grappling techniqes of *jū-jutsu* are a form of *bugei*, while the competitive and sporting *jūdō* is *budō*, having taken certain aspects of *jū-jutsu* as its starting-point. *Kenjutsu* teaches sword techniques using wooden *bokutō* in *kata*, while *kendō* practitioners fight with *shinai* in a way that is very different from the behaviour of a real sword, or even *shinai* use during the early Edo Period, where there were no restrictions on targets.

Modern *budō* also customarily uses a ranking system based on a series of pupil grades (*kyū*) and teacher grades (*dan*), denoted in many cases by the wearing of different coloured belts. Existing *bugei* stay with the *menkyo* system of 'licence to teach', which arises from the traditions concerned with passing on a *ryū's* secrets mentioned in an early chapter. There are still several existing *bugei-ryū* in Japan, such as the Maniwa Nen-ryū and the Tenshin Shōden Shintō-ryū, both of which have managed to preserve their traditions and avoid the 'sports' element of modern *budō*. Their students practise in a way that would have been very familiar to *sensei* such as Chiba Shūsaku.

Budō, of course, is far more popular, having left the rigours of *bugei* far behind. Not that I am seeking to condemn modern *budō*, far from it. It can be argued that if the modern *-dō* forms had not been created the martial arts would have died out completely. *Bugei* were designed for training combat swordsmen in as near to realistic conditions as possible. Mass participation in ancient *bugei* forms would be totally inappropriate, and while it is pleasing to note that there are still bands of enthusiasts, usually centred around a descendant of the *ryū's* founder, who keep these traditions alive, to some extent they are little more than valuable and interesting living fossils. Modern *budō* such as *karate* or *aikidō*, practised sincerely and with a sensitivity to their history and origins, are for most people the best expression of the martial arts ethos for the twentieth century. They provide fitness, comradeship and the satisfaction of success in skills that have to be practised to perfection.

▶ **Kendō** The present-day sport of *kendō* uses protective armour very similar to that developed during the eighteenth century. These combatants form a pair of bronze figurines. (Courtesy of Sotheby and Co.)

BUGEI AND BUDO

They also provide a genuine link with the past which can be very rewarding. It is only when the differences between old and new forms are forgotten that problems arise, and followers of a particular style argue for the 'purity' of their own interpretation, or cling stubbornly to a supposedly ancient tradition which may not be more than half a century old.

Bugei during the early Edo Period

The notion of martial arts as something divorced from real combat, or even practised as a sport, would have been totally unintelligible to a samurai of the Sengoku Period. Writers such as Kōsaka Danjō had a very simple and straightforward idea of what constituted the values of *bushidō*, and it is not surprising to find such down to earth sentiments applied to *bugei* as well. To a fighting samurai the value of *bugei* was totally without question, the only real argument being whether or not a samurai could learn anything of value in terms of swordsmanship off the battlefield. Kōsaka, of course, maintained that one could not. Only in the conditions of warfare could techniques be perfected. But perhaps this is a difference of perception, that the pragmatic Kōsaka failed to recognize the possibility that there could be a spiritual or moral dimension to swordsmanship. After all, as we saw in the chapter on the great *sensei*, Itō Ittōsai totally rejected any spiritual aspect to swordsmanship. To him the only 'perfection' one could attain was a technical perfection in the wielding of a sword, while the rival school of the Yagyū sought for a deeper insight. How strange that the early Tokugawa Shoguns should have received such contradictory opinions from their tutors!

The first of the Tokugawa to receive training from the Yagyū family was the first Tokugawa Shogun, Ieyasu, who, as well as dispensing 'benevolence' to his subjects, provided an excellent practical example of how in times of war theoretical notions of *bushidō* had to go hand-in-hand with practical skills in the martial arts. He was very interested in swords, swordsmanship and *bugei* in general. He swam regularly in the moats of Edo castle until he was in his seventies, and was a good shot with bow and gun, both of which he practised daily. Ieyasu was also very strong, which he once demonstrated by shooting a crane off one of the towers of Hamamatsu castle using the heavy form of arquebus known as a 'wall

▶ **An arm lock A sketch by Hokusai showing a lock applied to the arm. The arm is extended by pulling the victim forward, and pressure is applied against the elbow joint. Very similar locks are used in modern *aikidō*.**

gun', which would normally need extra support for its weight.

Even though Ieyasu had been a commander of samurai from an early age, on many occasions during his early career his life was saved by his own skills, rather than those of another. At the Battle of Azukizaka in 1563, one of Ieyasu's many tussles with the Buddhist fanatics of the Ikkō-ikki, an arrow was fired at him. He charged his horse full-tilt at the samurai who had discharged it, swinging his spear. The archer pulled his horse round and fled, but Ieyasu managed to get two swings in at him, slashing deep cuts into the back of his armour. He was also in receipt of a more modern form of missile, as was shown when he returned to Okazaki and took his armour off. As he loosened the tying cords two bullets fell out of his shirt. Ieyasu was also very sensitive to the prowess of others, and gave praise when it was due. At the Battle of the Anegawa in 1570 he commented upon the swordfighting skills of Okudaira Nobumasa, and added that good *kenjutsu* was a question of skill and not strength. He once interviewed the *kengō* Hikita Bungorō, Kamiizumi Nobutsuna's nephew, whom he criticized for his lack of appreciation that not everyone needed sword-fighting skills. For a *daimyō*, according to Ieyasu, the important thing was to know how to choose men who would do the fighting for him. A *daimyō* should not take risks. These opinions were of course delivered at a much later date in Ieyasu's life than the dramatic incidents described above, when Ieyasu had risked the future of his family more daringly than many of his less fortunate contemporaries.

The martial arts expand

Such sentiments dominated the thinking regarding martial arts until the early 1700s, when we begin to see the emergence of the use of *dō* (the way) in describing a training for martial arts that involved the human qualities as well as mere technical skills, thus anticipating the later use of the character *-dō* for the martial arts divorced from fighting. But *bugei* now had one additional important function to perform. In the same way as the possession

of two swords indicated membership of the samurai class, so prowess at *bugei*, and *kenjutsu* in particular, became regarded as a badge of rank, a corpus of knowledge and skill that lifted the samurai above the common herd. This notion, of course, only began to take form once it was perceived that the common herd were actually trying martial arts themselves.

By the beginning of the eighteenth century the lack of need for actual warlike skills meant that the martial arts could be more freely available to the lower classes, many of whom had already taken steps in that direction. While thinkers like Yamaga Sokō strove to fill the warrior's mind with noble thoughts about his calling in life, numerous *sensei* in their schools continued to attract aspiring young martial artists. The number of *ryū* multiplied, bringing to them many students, and much-needed income, from non-samurai classes. This expansion of the martial arts in social terms, and also in the way they were performed and the philosophy behind them, became a new vehicle for a different expression of *bushidō* and *bugei* ideals. At the same time, while the

memories of war faded farther into the past, swordsmanship lost more and more of its original discipline. The *shinai* had now virtually replaced the *bokutō* in all but the most traditional of *dōjō*s, and the introduction of protective armour, similar to the *kendō* armour of today (which began in the Jikishinkage-ryū), was a further move away from the severe discipline of the naked blade. Gradually there was a reduced emphasis on *jutsu*, or techniques, and more on *dō*, whereby martial arts could be studied for their own sake. The final development, from *dō* to a practice indistinguishable from sport, was a trend that was only to appear in the twentieth century, leaving very few schools still practising the old *bugei*.

The Eighteen Bugei

'Armchair samurai' of the Edo Period had another pastime to put beside that of re-writing *bushidō*. This was the classification of the 'Eighteen Varieties of the Martial Arts'. One example from 1815 includes one or two very unfamiliar activities:

THE MARTIAL ARTS DURING THE EDO PERIOD

1.	*kyū*	archery
2.	*uma*	horsemanship
3.	*dakyū*	'polo'
4.	*kisha*	equestrian archery (*yabusame*)
5.	*suiba*	swimming a horse
6.	*suihei*	swimming
7.	*yari*	spear
8.	*kusari-gama*	sickle and chain
9.	*naginata*	curved halberd
10.	*ken*	sword
11.	*yawara*	grappling (*jū-jutsu*)
12.	*i-ai*	sword drawing
13.	*hojō*	roping
14.	*hana-neji*	baton
15.	*yoroi-gumi*	grappling in armour
16.	*shūriken*	throwing weapons
17.	*sekkiya*	gunnery
18.	*teppō*	firearms

Various *ryū* tended to specialize in whichever variety they taught. We will conclude this chapter with a look at the above list, and certain of its omissions.

Several separate techniques fall under the heading of 'horse and bow - *jutsu*'. *Dakyū*, the Japanese equivalent of polo, was introduced from China, and from illustrations of people performing *dakyū* it looks somewhat more like a form of mounted lacrosse. Although of obvious use as a form of training for a man wielding a spear from horseback, *dakyū* was never very popular. It was played between two teams of seven men, each of whom carried in his net a ball of the same distinctive colour as his team's costume. The object of the game was for each member of the team to throw his ball into a goal set up in the middle of the field, which consisted of a netting bag inside a wooden screen. The winning team was the first to get all seven balls into the net.

Yabusame was mentioned in connection with the Gempei Period, and unlike *dakyū* has remained a recognized martial accomplishment still performed at certain festivals today. It is very spectacular to watch, as the archers, dressed in hunting gear, fire their humming-bulb arrows at small targets. Similar to *yabusame*, but more difficult to perform, was a training exercise and sport that does not appear in the above list called *inu-oi*,

THE GRAPPLING ARTS

▲ **Dog shooting** A drawing from a 'Lone Wolf' episode. (Lone Wolf and Cub © 1989 First Publishing Inc. and Global Communications Corp)

◄ **The eighteen varieties of the martial arts** An unusual, but sadly poor quality, woodblock print showing one version of the eighteen martial arts.

'dog-shooting'. Shooting dogs with the bow trained a mounted archer in hitting a moving target, and was apparently very popular with the Hōjō family of Odawara in the sixteenth century. During the Edo Period it provided an alternative to hunting. The dog was released from within a small roped circle. The archer would canter round the outside of the circle, inside a further roped enclosure. Once the dog was free it would try to escape,

and the archer had to shoot it before it passed either the outer or the inner boundary.

The grappling arts

Sumō, associated in the West with the huge professional wrestlers, has always had an amateur following among those who are much less heavy. The *kengō* Chiba Shūsaku was very good at *sumō*. It was not a 'martial art' as such, and foreign enthusiasm for Japanese grappling has been largely confined to offshoots of *jū-jutsu*, though this may well change now that *sumō* can be seen on Western television.

Yawara and *jū-jutsu* are two expressions for the grappling arts, which include those performed in armour as *yoroi-gumi*, an important fighting skill during the

THE MARTIAL ARTS DURING THE EDO PERIOD

▲ **Horse techniques** A sketch by Hokusai showing *yabusame* and *dakyū*, the Japanese version of polo.

a small *kozuka* knife thrust through his sleeve as a friendly warning and confirmation of his *sensei's* tremendous skills. One of the Yagyū family was also skilled at *jū-jutsu*, and in the year 1624 was umpire at a match when one of the contestants challenged him to a contest. Yagyū declined, at which the man became angry, so Yagyū promptly swept the man off his feet, giving him his contest in style! Another later master, Terada Goemon, being commanded to bow before the procession of the Mito *daimyō*, refused to do so until the actual

▶ **Sumō wrestling** A woodblock print by Kuniyoshi showing how little *sumō* has changed over the years.

▼ **A master of *jū-jutsu*** Sekiguchu Jūshi was an expert at *jū-jutsu*, which he demonstrated on one occasion on his own *daimyō* when the young lord sought to test him.

Gempei War, described in detail earlier in this book. During the Edo Period armoured grappling declined greatly, to be replaced by the techniques more familiar today. The essence of *jū*, which is the Chinese reading of the character *yawara*, is the use of an opponent's strength against himself, a principle often forgotten in modern *budō* and sports versions of the grappling arts.

Masters of *jū-jutsu* were almost as highly regarded as master swordsmen, and there are several stories told about them. One such concerns Sekiguchi Jūshin, whose employing *daimyō*, to try him out, tried to push him off the edge of a bridge. Sekiguchi sidestepped, and the young lord found himself dangling almost in mid-air, with

源の昌景妹の
孝子平吉が
歎きも
山さんと純音
山の

男水滸傳豪傑ノ壹個

做し関取角力進
投精神倍盛ありそと
礒兵衛朝花川とあらつく
夜叉山嵐や取組土俵の真中に
地響させく

THE MARTIAL ARTS DURING THE EDO PERIOD

◀ Time, gentlemen, please! A bartender in Yokohama prepares to clear the establishment of drunken sailors. Incidents like this in the treaty ports often led to a Westerner's first appreciation of the skills of *jū-jutsu*.

daimyō's palanquin came in sight. He explained that he had chanced upon the procession by mistake, and that to prostrate himself before fellow samurai was not in keeping with his rank. The enraged samurai attendants tried to seize him, and by the time the lord's palanquin did arrive he had put six armed men on their backs.

Jū-jutsu came to the attention of the West when rowdy sailors felt the force of it in the treaty ports. Rudyard Kipling made a famous comment upon *jū-jutsu* in an article in *The Times* of 1892, referring specifically to the use of it against drunken British seamen:

'. . . he has a grievance against the Japanese policeman (all Japanese policemen are required to have a workable knowledge of Judo [*sic*]) who is paid a dollar for every strayed seaman he brings up to the Consular Courts for overstaying his leave and so forth. Jack says that the little fellows deliberately hinder him from getting back on his ship, and then, with devilish art and craft of wrestling tricks - "there are about a hundred of 'em and they can throw you with every qualified one" - carry him to justice.'

Jū-jutsu does not necessarily imply purely unarmed combat, which is how it has tended to evolve nowadays. Many weapons were used, such as *tantō* and chain weapons. *Kusari-gama* was the technique of using the fearsome sickle and chain. As we noted earlier, Miyamoto Musashi overcame one by throwing a *shūriken*, and Araki Mata'emon of the Yagyū Shinkage-ryū defeated an opponent whirling a *kusari-gama* by the sensible expedient of walking slowly backwards until the duel ended up in a dense bamboo grove. The *manriki-kusari* or 'thousand power chain', consisted of a forged iron chain with a counterweight at each end, which was flung from the hand, or swung.

◀ *Hana-neji* The martial art of *hana-neji* 'nose-twisting' using the form of short baton otherwise employed to control an unruly horse. It is the forerunner of modern police baton techniques.

Hana-neji, when literally translated, has the alarming meaning of 'nose-twisting'. The nose, however, is that of an unruly horse, and it was apparently the custom to control an unruly animal by placing a loop of cord through its nostrils. When it became troublesome a short baton was inserted in the loop and the horse's nose was given a good twist! The baton so used was also found useful as a primitive form of policeman's truncheon, though not, curiously enough by the *dōshin*, who preferred their steel *jitte*, the traditional sword-catchers. The techniques were however used by *yōjimbo* as an alternative to their *bō*, and may be regarded as a direct forerunner of the Japanese riot policeman's baton.

The biggest controversy surrounding the history of grappling arts centres around the relationship between *jū-jutsu* and *jūdō*. *Jūdō*, the name given by Jigoro Kano to his own corpus of grappling techniques, has all but swamped *jū-jutsu* in the popular mind. Present-day students of *jū-jutsu* claim that this was done deliberately, and that the early history of Judo was rewritten to make it appear more like a natural progression from old *jū-jutsu* forms, creating the popular myth that Kano saved *jū-jutsu* by making it into Judo. Even Kano's noble motivation is questioned. It is claimed that Judo was never seen purely as a contribution to education and physical training, but as a means of maintaining the combat skills of the nation's youth for any war that was to come. There is no space here to comment upon such arguments, but it is interesting to note that *jū-jutsu* is one of the few surviving *bugei* forms to be practised at all in the West. Some of the most successful *budō* off-shoots of *jū-jutsu* have a comparatively short history. *Aikidō*, for instance, effectively dates from 1942, and its sports variety, founded by Tomiki, is even younger. All these activities, however, have very respectable and ancient origins, and by sincere and dedicated practice one is allowed a unique link with the *bugei* of the past, with *bushidō* and with the person of the lone samurai.

Throwing weapons

Throwing weapons have never been much used in Japan. There is no equivalent to the javelin, for example. The well-known *shūriken*, favourite of the *ninja*, began as a crude art of throwing by samurai, with weapons ranging from *tantō* to *wakizashi*. In the *Taiheiki* a certain samurai had 'thirty-six large arrows carried on his back, which he

▲ **The use of the *jō*** A page from the Hokusai sketchbook showing techniques of *jō-jutsu*.

---

threw by hand at the enemy and pierced them . . .' Specially manufactured *uchine* or throwing arrows followed. There are not many cases of throwing a *wakizashi*, however, but one occurs in the *Ōsaka gunki*: 'Ogasawara Tadamasa was the keeper of Akaseki Castle; when the enemy arrived he was pierced with a spear through the *mune-ita* of his armour. He threw his *wakizashi* as a *shūriken* and made his escape.' There is a similar illustration in the *Jōzan Kidan*. In 1574 Takeda Katsuyori was about to capture a castle from Suganuma Sadamitsu. The Suganuma family had been betrayed to the Takeda and the fall of the castle was inevitable, so a council of war decided to break off the fighting, but for a castle commander to escape would be dishonourable for any wielder of bow and arrow, so he did not agree at first. By now the enemy were close at hand, and had set fire to the castle. At the very last moment Suganuma went off with Yamaguchi Gorōsaku and one other close associate on three horses, hotly pursued by the Takeda. They fired their two remaining arrows, and as a last resort Gorōsaku drew the *wakizashi* which he had with him, and threw it as a *shūriken*. It skimmed over the samurai's head, and Gorōsaku was killed.

A battle of the Sengoku Period gave little scope for unconventional techniques to be developed, but in the dark streets of Edo such things as the *shūriken* came into their own. There is a marvellous demonstration of *shūriken* throwing in the film *Yōjimbō*, when one is thrown and stops the firing of a pistol.

The old chronicles contain numerous references to the techniques of swimming with horses, particularly when crossing a river to start a battle. The best known occur at the three separate battles fought at Uji, when horse-swimming was a means of gaining the supreme honour of being first into battle. At the 1184 battle two samurai competed to be first across. When half-way across the eventual winner hindered the other by telling him that his saddle-girth was loose. Swimming while armoured, helped by floats, was another accomplishment. Some skilled swimmers could fire a bow and arrow from a floating position!

Different compilers of the 'eighteen varieties' made different lists. Some include the war-fan, which was best demonstrated by Takeda Shingen when he used it to defend himself against his rival Uesugi Kenshin's surprise attack at the Fourth Battle of Kawanakajima. We may also note the *jō*, a shorter form of the longer staff called the *bō* as used by the *yōjimbō*. Its invention is credited to a warrior called Muso Gonosuke, who had been defeated by Miyamoto Musashi. Muso meditated on his defeat and conceived the idea of using a short staff which could be rotated easily, using both ends with which to strike. On their subsequent encounter he managed to stop Musashi from striking him, which was no mean feat. The *jō* is a fascinating weapon to watch in action, as its *jōdō* techniques include various strikes and catches.

Other lists of the martial arts include the most controversial discipline of all, *ninjutsu*, the techniques of stealth and invisibility. The nature of *ninjutsu*, and its practitioners, the *ninja*, is such a vast subject that we will devote the following chapter exclusively to it.

11.

Ninja - the Invisible Lone Warrior

No category of 'lone warrior' has received more attention in recent times than the mysterious, black-clad 'super-samurai' called *ninja*, performing the mysterious and deadly martial art of *ninjutsu*. Nor is any aspect of *bugei* more shrouded in mystery, or more abused by claims made about it. Present-day practitioners speak of it as a surviving *bugei* form, which is an astonishing claim to make for a corpus of techniques involving assassination. In this chapter I intend to take a critical look at this aspect of martial behaviour, although it is impossible to do justice to such a vast subject in a brief account.

The common reading of the word *ninja*, simply enough, means 'invisible man', and *ninjutsu* means the 'art of invisibility', or more usually, 'the art of stealth'. In essence the historical figure whose activities have given rise to the *ninja* myth is an undercover agent, carrying out the functions of spy, intelligence gatherer and assassin. During the Sengoku Period in particular such techniques were well-used on campaign, and included *sekkō* (spy) and *kanchō* (espionage) techniques and skills. The historical use of the words *ninja* and *ninjutsu* is itself interesting, because what we now call *ninjutsu* was originally called *shinobi-no-jutsu*, *Shinobi* being merely the alternative reading of the character *nin*, hence the use of the word *shinobi no mono* rather than *ninja* in old accounts.

There were in fact many other words used for the individuals who employed these undercover techniques, and they appear in many of the old chronicles. The *Kōyō Gunkan* calls them *kagimono-hiki*, a good name for spies as it literally means 'sniffing and hearing', and in one chapter of the *Hōjō Godai-ki* they are referred to as *kusa*, or 'grass', probably because as spies they spent a lot of time lying down in long grass near an enemy's lines. Alternatively they can be referred to in terms of the actual activities to which *shinobi* were put, including *kanchō* (spies) in enemy provinces, and in times of war *teisatsu* (scouts), *kishū* (surprise attacks), and *kōran* (agitators). For convenience I shall use the word *ninja* in this chapter for all these categories, and *ninjutsu* for the techniques, except where the contemporary context is different.

There has been much discussion in recent years concerning the time when the word *ninja* rather than *shinobi*, began to be used. To some extent this is a fruitless argument, because several names were used during the Sengoku Period, as noted above. It is however,

NINJA – THE INVISIBLE LONE WARRIOR

▲ **Modern *ninjutsu* techniques are demonstrated by a student of the modern practitioner Dr. Masaaki Hatsumi.**

more than likely that the reading as *ninja*, which trips more readily off a Western tongue, is a fairly modern phenomenon. It is important to note, however, that the use of the word *ninja* for the practitioners of undercover work implies that various loosely connected activities are attributed exclusively to a particular *group* of individuals, rather than being merely a set of techniques (*ninjutsu*), performed by anyone so trained, such as *ashigaru* sent on spying missions, local farmers hired for a reconnaissance vigil, etc. To speak of such activities as carried out by *ninja* implies a caste, a 'secret society', and the development of what might be termed the '*ninja* cult'.

Early ninjutsu

As various undercover operations are fundamental to the conduct of war in any culture, it is not surprising to read of such techniques being used throughout Japanese history, but there would appear to be little historical justification for the claims advanced by modern-day practitioners of *ninjutsu* that theirs is a martial art dedicated to self-fulfillment and the training of mind and body. In Japanese history *ninjutsu*, whatever its practitioners were called, was both undercover and underhand. Furthermore despite the obvious advantages *ninja* brought to a *daimyō* whose dirty work they did, their craft was often thoroughly despised. Some of the early accounts, examples of which follow, do however speak in tones of admiration concerning such activities. One of the earliest incidents of all, which was mentioned in the first chapter of this book, is described in a very matter-of-fact way as an obvious accomplishment by a skilled warrior. This is of course the story of Prince Yamato, who disguised himself as a girl in order to gain admittance to the headquarters of the enemy chieftain he was hunting. He had a sword concealed in his dress, and when the merrymaking reached its height he drew the sword and

▲ **Ninja!** Four modern lady *ninja*, who act as guides to the museum, pose for the camera at Iga Ueno. Ueno is the centre for modern interest in, and study of, *ninjutsu*.

stabbed the chieftain, as classic an account of a *ninjutsu* operation as one is likely to read anywhere. Prince Yamato, of course, is nowhere referred to as a *ninja*, but the tone of the account suggests a praiseworthy act, and, more importantly, the use of a technique that had been learned and perfected.

The branch of *ninjutsu* techniques known as *kanchō* appears in the earliest of the *gunkimono*, or 'war tales', the historical and military romances that are our main source for the fighting techniques of the Heian and Kamakura Periods. It is a brief mention, but fascinating in that it reminds us forcibly of one other aspect of undercover techniques, that to a 'regular soldier' in any culture, such operations have never been generally admired. In the *Shōmonki*, the earliest war chronicle, which deals with the life of Taira Masakado and which

was probably completed shortly after his death in AD 940, we hear of spies being dispatched to the enemy camp; then we read simply: 'Over forty of the enemy were killed on that day, and only a handful managed to escape with their lives. Those who were able to survive the fighting fled in all directions, blessed by Heaven's good fortune. As for Yoshikane's spy Koharumaru, Heaven soon visited its punishment upon him; his misdeeds were found out, and he was captured and killed on the 23rd day of the First Month, Jōhei 8.'

I have been able to find no reference to undercover operations, beyond a straightforward use of scouts, in either of the two great war tales the *Hōgen Monogatari*, and the *Heike Monogatari* which we used in early chapters. Perhaps this is not so surprising because these classics were written for an aristocratic audience who wished to hear of the glorious deeds of their ancestors, and the whole tone of the works is that of a litany of the performance of great men. The activities of the common footsoldiers, who outnumbered the mounted samurai by

NINJA – THE INVISIBLE LONE WARRIOR

twenty to one in the armies of the time, are almost totally ignored, so it is perhaps only to be expected that ignoble undercover acts are conspicuous by their absence. The one exception is the story that begins the *Heike Monogatari*, when Taira Tadamori thwarts an attempt to assassinate him by using the sort of trick later attributed to skilled *ninja*. Being warned beforehand that rivals in the Court intended his death: '. . . he provided himself with a long *tantō* which he girt on under his long court dress, and turning aside to a dimly lit place, slowly drew the blade, and passed it through the hair of his head so that it gleamed afar with an icy sheen, causing all to stare open-eyed.' The bringing of weapons within the presence of the Emperor was a serious offence, and Tadamori was ordered to give an account of himself, whereupon: '. . . they hastened to bring forth the sword and exhibit it. Its outside was that of a dirk in a black lacquer sheath, but within was only a wooden blade covered with silver. Although he had displayed the appearance of a sword to

avoid dishonour, his substitution of a wooden blade was exceedingly praiseworthy. A plan like this is very commendable in a warrior.' In other words the use of a *ninjutsu* technique is approved of in such circumstances.

It has been claimed that the later war tale the *Taiheiki* contains references to undercover operations being carried out by *shinobi*. For example, the following fragment is quoted by Sasama as the earliest written account of a *shinobi* assassination: '. . . Saburō's chest was pierced with a sword. His guards heard a strange sound, took a torch from the fire and hurried up to see Homma Saburō in his bedroom with blood pouring out of him. Saburō-*dono* had been injured by a malicious *shinobi* . . .' However, a careful reading of the original text dispels any image of a black-clad assassin sneaking

▼ **A *ninja* device** An illustration from the seventeenth-century *ninja* treatise entitled *Bansen Shūkai*, depicting various grapnel hooks.

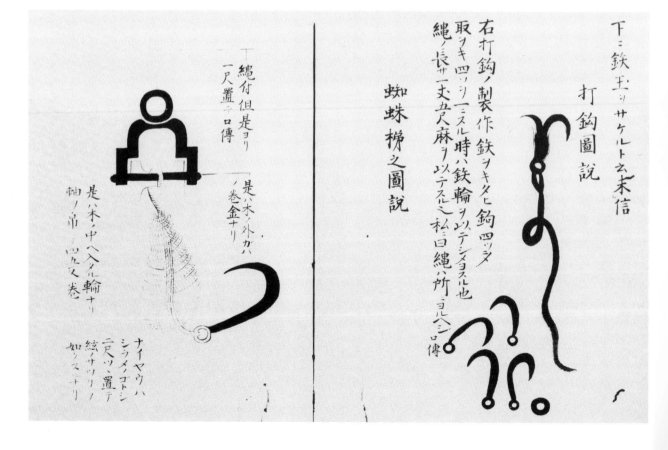

THE AKAMATSU MURDERS

into Homma Saburō's room under cover of darkness, because the assassin was a twelve-year-old boy, whose father, exiled to the island of Sado, had been executed by this Homma Saburō. The boy had joined his father in exile, and was to be sent back to the mainland, but he feigned illness and was allowed to stay on Sado. That night he crept along the corridor outside Saburō's room, bursting for revenge, but obviously totally unprepared as he had no weapon. Seeing the murderer of his father lying asleep he realized what an opportunity had presented itself, so he calmly drew Saburō's sword from the scabbard that lay beside his bed, and plunged it into his chest. The youth, called Kumawaka, may not have been a 'professional' *ninja*, but the story lacks none of the flavour because of it. There is a further neat little *ninja* touch whereby Kumawaka douses the light in Saburō's bedroom by opening the window and letting insects swarm in on to it.

But *shinobi* techniques were not infallible. In an obscure work entitled *Yoshōki* (which may not have been compiled until the seventeenth century) we read: 'In 1367 . . . on the eleventh day of the same month Tadaoka Rokugorō Saemon knocked down a *shinobi* who had entered Ototsu castle.' There are a few other references from the time of the Nambokuchō Wars, some concerning Kusunoki Masashige's defence of Chihaya and Akasaka, when samurai climbed in undetected.

The Akamatsu murders

The period of uneasy peace which followed the union of the Northern and Southern Courts in 1392 under Yoshi-mitsu ended with a classic case of *shinobi* assassination which has all the hallmarks of the undercover work later to be attributed to *ninja*. This was the so called Kakitsu Affair of 1441, of which the victim of the assassination was the Shogun Ashikaga Yoshinori. His enemy Akamatsu Mitsusuke invited the Shogun to visit his Kyōto mansion under the pretext of celebrating a recent victory against the Yūki. Yoshinori had feasted well and was enjoying a performance of dancing when a herd of horses broke loose into the garden. Large numbers of armed

◄ **A *ninja* scales a wall** A model of a *ninja* in the museum at Iga-Ueno. This is the traditional image of the secretive *ninja* attack.

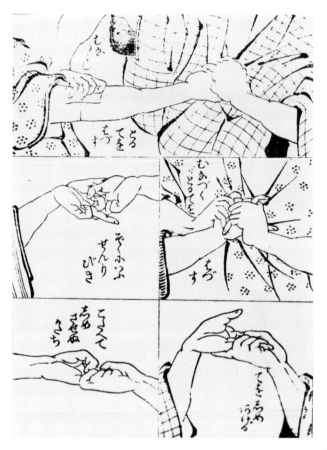

▲ *Jū-jutsu* grips The techniques of unarmed grappling were a vital part of *ninja* lore. This is a page of arm and wrist locks from Hokusai's sketchbooks.

warriors appeared, ostensibly to seal off the garden and round up the horses, but in the confusion the Shogun was set upon and murdered. There is no suggestion that any people resembling *ninja* had anything to do with this incident. It was all planned by Akamatsu Mitsusuke, a very respectable samurai! There is a tendency, however, for any such operation to be called a '*ninja* attack' in modern written accounts of it. For instance, the subsequent operation of 1458, whereby the treacherous Akamatsu were restored to the incumbent Shogun's favour, is an interesting example of how such an affair can be made into a '*ninja* assassination' by a modern commentator.

Following the union of the Courts there were a number

of attempts by erstwhile Southern Court supporters to reopen their claim to the throne. One of the more successful had taken place in 1443, when an attack was launched on the Imperial Palace. The assailants escaped with two of the items of Imperial Regalia - the sword and the jewels. The sword was quickly recovered before it had left the capital, but the jewels were taken deep into the Yoshino mountains where the 'Southern Pretender' held court. His supporters held out for nearly fifteen years, until in 1458 a group of Akamatsu Mitsusuke's former retainers requested service at the pretender's court. As their former master had murdered a rival Shogun they were accepted with no suspicion, but on a snowy night in the twelfth month they killed the 'Southern Emperor' and escaped with the jewels. A colourful addition to the story is that in order to speed their progress over the Obagamine Pass they buried the pretender's severed head in the snow. intending to return for it later, but that the blood seeping from it into the snow gave away its presence to their pursuers. The Akamatsu samurai eventually succeeded in returning with the jewels to Kyōto, and obtained an official pardon for the Akamatsu in 1459. Such is the story of the Akamatsu raid. I visited the area in 1986, and in preparation for my walk through the Odaigahara mountains I purchased detailed maps of the area, and there is a reference in the notes to the Akamatsu attack on the Southern Emperor's hideout. The notes identify the location and state simply that the attack was carried out by six *ninja*, a word not used in the primary source, nor in any of the three references to the incident available in English!

The ninja of Iga

One of the most common references to *ninja* in popular works is concerned with the so-called *ninja* families of Iga Province. According to Sasama, by about 1487 the use as mercenaries of *shinobi* from Iga was well-established. In the *Tamon-In nikki*, which is a very reliable source in the form of a diary kept by a priest of the Tamon-In, a sub-temple of the Kōfuku-ji at Nara, we read: 'This morning, the sixth day of the eleventh month of 1541, a few of the Iga-*shū* entered Kasagi castle in secret and set fire to the priest's quarters, also in several places they set fire to outbuildings . . .' Interestingly, the famous Yagyū family, who later founded the Yagyū Shinkage-ryū,

▲ **Ladies' weapons** A page by Hokusai showing *kusari-gama* and *naginata*.

were involved in this battle, and there has been much speculation as to whether or not the Yagyū were also involved in *ninjutsu*. They certainly lived in the vicinity of the traditional *ninja* heartlands, and little is known of their actual involvement in the Battle of Sekigahara, at which time they were firmly in the service of the Tokugawa. Whatever service they performed was richly rewarded after the battle in terms of a considerable increase in revenue, so perhaps they were engaged upon some secret operation? Yagyū Jūbei Mitsuyoshi, the third *sensei* of the *Yagyū Shinkage-ryū*, is said to have acted as a spy for the Shogun Tokugawa Iemitsu. We noted earlier, too, that according to legend Tsukahara Bokuden's son became a *ninja* after the death of his guardian Kitabatake Tomonori.

But not all *ninja* were so respectable. Sasama distinguishes between the expert *shinobi*, who passed on their traditions to their descendants, of which the Iga-*shū* are the best example, and others who were no more than bandits, hired temporarily as *kanchō*. He adds that *shinobi* were time and again misunderstood and mistrusted by their own allies, and that *shinobi* techniques were perceived as no more than theft. However, when taken along within an army *shinobi* were treated as personal attendants serving in an expert occupation. Finally, as the Tokugawa had rules for just about everything in life, it is not surprising to find regulations covering the use of such persons. In 1649, in the *bakufu's* laws for military service, only those of 10,000 *koku* and above were allowed to be accompanied by *shinobi* when they went to war.

The ninja become larger than life

Given the existence of such factual accounts, it may seem unnecessary to embellish what is already a fascinating tradition. Yet legends grow, leading to the superhuman *ninja* figure of today, but what is most remarkable is that this 'tradition' of making the *ninja* considerably larger than life has a very long history indeed. The first trend one can discern is that of associating *shinobi* and *ninjutsu* with famous warriors who are historical personages, but who at some time in their careers led a mysterious or fugitive life. The two great heroes Minamoto Yoshitsune (1159—89) and Kusunoki Masashige (1294—1336) are the ones most often mentioned, to the extent that they are sometimes credited in popular works with the foundation of two separate 'schools of *ninjutsu*', the Yoshitsune-ryū and the Kusunoki-ryū.

The second identifiable trend is to link the *ninja* with the sect of wandering friars called *yamabushi*, 'those who lie down in mountains'. At first sight *ninja* and *yamabushi* seem to have little in common apart from their inherent mystery, yet the guise of a wandering *yamabushi* was the ideal cover for a role that involved espionage and travel, and we know that some *yamabushi* themselves acted as spies for rival *daimyō*.

The third trend is to credit *ninja* with their own mysterious powers, independent of any other association. A classic example, which shows how old is the tradition of embellishment, is that of Nakagawa

Shōshunjin, who lived about 1672. The most fascinating account of his life includes the words '. . . he could change into a rat or a spider, and transform himself into birds and animals . . .', a neat illustration of the power attributed to *ninja*, and showing that *ninja* were already perceived as supermen by the end of the seventeenth century. In reality Nakagawa Shōshunjin had the command of a group of ten young samurai who practised *ninjutsu*, and he forbade any other men from coming near the place where they practised, which was at the southern corner of the castle. In conclusion there is no shortage of reference in the old chronicles to *ninja*-like activities, and a very old tradition of making them larger than life. *Ninja* are far from being a modern invention. But how authentic are the much acclaimed *ninjutsu* techniques?

The fighting arts of the ninja

One of the most obviously necessary 'fighting arts' of the *ninja* is the one that is most often ignored in popular accounts, that of disguise. It would seem unlikely that a *ninja* spent much of his 'working life' dressed from head to foot in black. Most accounts of *shinobi* operations imply the use of disguise so that the spy or assassin could mingle with his surroundings. A *yamabushi* was a useful identity to adopt, as mentioned above, or even that of a simple farmer would suffice. In Kurosawa's film *Kagemusha* these are the guises adopted by the Oda and Tokugawa agents sent to discover whether or not Takeda Shingen is dead. They wander freely through the streets of the town, unremarkable to any passer-by.

The *ninja* would of course be as highly skilled as any samurai in the standard martial arts of bow, spear and sword, and the grappling arts of *jū-jutsu*, but he would be particularly expert in the field of concealed weaponry, including fearsome-looking *shuko* (knuckle-dusters). There was also a vast range of *shūriken* available to him, ranging from small knives to tiny darts, as well as the notorious 'ninja stars', the curious, and probably wildly inaccurate throwing weapons spun out of the fingers at

a pursuer. Apparently during the filming of the James Bond film *You Only Live Twice* in the mid-1960s, which for many in the West was the first they had ever heard or seen of *ninja*, complaints were laid against the film company by the local council who owned Himeji castle.

▶ **A *yamabushi*** The *ninja* are often associated with the wandering priests called *yamabushi*, which was a popular disguise for a spy. These present-day *yamabushi* are from the Shōgō-In in Kyōto.

THE FIGHTING ARTS OF THE NINJA

Himeji was the location of a memorable sequence of *ninja* in action, and as the castle had recently been expensively restored to its feudal grandeur the authorities were greatly concerned at the damage being done to its woodwork by flying *shūriken!*

Tetsu-bishi, or caltrops, were useful little devices to drop when being pursued. Although not a *ninja* invention (their use is universal and goes back to ancient times), the cluster of metal spikes that always had one point vertical were a particularly useful hindrance in a culture

NINJA – THE INVISIBLE LONE WARRIOR

▲ *Shūriken* **practice** A sketch by Hokusai of practice with the dart-like versions of *shūriken*, using a target with a face painted on it.

that wore only straw sandals on its feet. *Kusari-gama*, the sickle with a chain, and various poles with hooks, chains and concealed knives also appeared in the *ninja* armoury. A curious telescopic spear which could be extended by operating a simple mechanism was also used, but apparently not exclusively by *ninja*. Add to this list poisons, blinding pepper powder, river-crossing devices and collapsible ladders and you have the perfect amalgam of martial art and mystery that has made the *ninja* the popular subject he is today.

There is much more that could be said about authenticated *ninja* assassinations, raids on castles and undercover work in general, but let us conclude this brief survey with my favourite *ninja* story, which, as far as I am aware, has never before been translated into English. It is supposed to be a true incident, and concerns a raid on a house by two very skilled *ninja*. On entering the house they were disturbed by the guards and withdrew. One climbed back over the garden wall, but the other concealed himself in a tree in the garden. When he did not appear for some time his companion became worried about him and re-entered the garden. Creeping up to the tree he called up into the branches, in as loud a whisper as he dared, that the guards had gone and that it was now safe to come down and escape. But the man up the tree, being, naturally, a highly trained and skilful *ninja*, had had it impressed upon him not to trust voices, lest it be an enemy mimicking the voice of a friend. So he stayed motionless in the branches and ignored his companion's increasingly desperate pleas. The *ninja* on the ground then noticed to his horror that the guards were starting to stir again, and realized that there was only one way to ensure that his comrade came down from the tree and escaped. He turned towards the house, and shouted at the top of his voice, 'There's a *ninja* up the tree!', at which point, of course, his companion leapt down to the ground and fled over the garden wall!

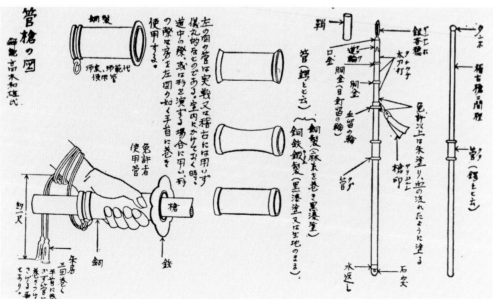

◀ A *kuda-yari* A *ninja*-like weapon, which consisted of a long spear, telescoped inside a short shaft, which could be ejected easily; the opponent having been fooled into thinking the spear was only a few feet long.

12.

The Last of the Swords- men

As was implied by the earlier chapter on *bushidō*, the greatest challenge facing the master swordsmen of the Tokugawa Period was the fact that wars had ceased, seemingly for ever, under the benevolent rule of the Shoguns. Not only did they establish peace, they also tried to cut Japan off from almost all contact with the outside world. No foreigner was allowed to land in Japan, and no Japanese was allowed to leave. The development of *bugei* and *bushidō* which we studied earlier therefore took place in a society isolated from almost every other nation.

By the mid-nineteenth century this policy, and the certainty of eternal peace, became increasingly questioned. Russia, America and England were expanding their interests in the East, and it looked very likely that one of these nations would soon try to make new contact with Japan. When it eventually came it threw the whole of Japanese society into turmoil, caused a revolution, and led to the emergence of modern Japan. The threat of Western intervention brought about the revival of *bugei* in a way that an encouragement to emulate Confucian values had never been able to achieve. Just as the Mongol invasions made Japan look at her preparations for defence, so the idleness and lack of skills bemoaned by writers such as Murata Seifu and Ogyū Sorai were flung suddenly into reverse. New *kengō* appeared, fired by a genuine desire to serve either the decaying Shogunate or the new underground movements which sought to restore the Emperor and expel the foreigners. One of the earliest manifestations of this was the enthusiasm for swordfighting displayed by a new generation of swordsmen who knew they would need good techniques for the inevitable war. The wheel of *bugei* had now almost turned full circle. Swordfighting had long since achieved its art form and left mere technique behind, but as the prospect of war came anew the art of the sword reverted to its original function as a device for killing people, and the gentle *shinai* prepared to give way to the naked blade.

The new sensei

The revival of the martial arts preceded the actual revolution by about thirty years, making the 1830s and 1840s the 'Indian Summer' of Japanese swordsmanship. *Sensei* arose who, in their fighting skills, and their unquestionable authority, equalled any from the Sengoku Period. The main difference between them and their

THE LAST OF THE SWORDSMEN

▲ *Kenjutsu* and *yari-jutsu* in a *dōjō* A section from the Hokusai sketchbooks.

predecessors was the lack of opportunity the later *sensei* had of demonstrating their skills with real swords. None could risk his life in a duel, or have the satisfaction of defeating an opponent with a devastating *hitotsu-tachi* stroke. Their techniques were confined to *i-ai*, *bokutō* or *shinai*, and consisted largely of *kata*. Nevertheless swordfighting enjoyed enormous popularity, and by the end of the Tokugawa Period there were seven hundred *ryū* in existence, and well-established schools such as the Yagyū Shinkage-ryū and the Ittō-ryū had split into several branches.

The *sensei* of these decades had one great advantage over the masters who were shortly to succeed them. The threat from foreign nations had led to an increased demand for their services, but it was unspoiled by the dark cloud that was to come later when revolution made

swordfighting a combat skill once again. One of the best examples of such a *sensei* at his imperious best is the story of the challenge made by a certain Shimada Tora-no-suke to the great *sensei* Otani Nobutomo, a man who exhibited all the personality of the earlier masters. Shimada Tora-no-suke was the son of Shimada Chikafusa, a samurai of the Nakatsu *han* of Buzen, who in 1837 at the age of twenty-four, went to Edo to seek his fortune.

His swordfighting skills were considerable, but so was his fiery temperament, and he created havoc in the Edo *dōjō*s when he challenged others to fierce bouts in which he seemed never to be defeated. This made the young Tora-no-suke very conceited, a personality weakness among swordsmen which we have noted several times in the past. He eventually challenged to a contest Otani Nobutomo, an older man, well-respected as a *sensei*, and who was regarded as being the best swordsman in Edo at the time.

THE NEW SENSEI

▲ Grappling in armour A warrior engages enemies in the techniques of *yoroi-gumi*, or armoured grappling, which in olden days was the usual style of close combat following an archery duel. The techniques of *jū-jutsu* can be traced back to such practices.

Nobutomo accepted the challenge, much to the disgust of his companions, who felt that the precocious Tora-no-suke was beneath their *sensei's* dignity. They fought with *bokutō*, and Nobutomo took the first blow. Tora-no-suke took the next blow from Nobutomo, then the third blow from Tora-no-suke hit Nobutomo beside the eye, and the contest was brought to a halt. Young Tora-no-suke, having received only one blow from Nobutomo, became more conceited than ever, and was convinced also that Nobutomo was not the great swordsman he had been told about. What Tora-no-suke did not know was that it was Nobutomo's custom to treat all aspiring young martial artists in this way. First he would let them gain an easy victory, to test how well they responded to the elation of success. Then there would be a re-match, and Nobutomo would give them a sound beating. Oblivious of this, Tora-no-suke went on to challenge others who had a less generous approach to young braggarts. Hearing of the reputation of a certain Inoue Gensai, Tora-

no-suke sought to challenge him to a contest, but Gensai reckoned that to be pitted against the sword of a rustic-trained countryman like Tora-no-suke was not consistent with his rank. Tora-no-suke then changed his tack, and asked if he could join his pupils, to which Gensai replied, 'I have achieved the highest standard of swordsmanship in Edo. A young person of promise like you would not be satisfied by an old master like me. However, there are in Edo men who would fulfil your requirements. Have you visited Otani-*sensei*?'

Gensai already knew what had happened when Tora-no-suke had visited Otani, and smiled to hear Tora-no-suke say, 'Oh, yes, I have visited him. Of three blows delivered only one was on me. I think he is a person of lesser skill than I.' 'Perhaps he did not fully appreciate your abilities as an opponent,' said Gensai. 'Let me give you an official letter of introduction to Otani-*sensei*. You can visit him once more.' Tora-no-suke took the letter of introduction and visited Otani for a second time, and as Gensai had anticipated, the results of their combat were very different. Tora-no-suke never succeeded in landing the slightest blow on Otani, who vanquished him utterly. By that defeat Tora-no-suke was enlightened, and it turned out that the experience taught him a very valuable lesson. It turned him towards a more realistic pursuit of knowledge, and instead of returning to Gensai, he became a pupil of Otani Nobutomo, who had already recognized that there was a latent talent behind all that bravado. Tora-no-suke stayed with Otani's school for the rest of his life.

Chiba Shūsaku

Another outstanding *sensei* of the 'Indian Summer' was Chiba Shūsaku, whose comments on contests between schools we noted earlier. He was the son of a former samurai doctor, and went to Edo from his home province at the age of sixteen in 1809. He joined the Ittō-ryū, but showed such talent that he eventually left and set up his own school, the Hokushin-Ittō-ryū. Here he studied under the *sensei* Takai Matashichirō, who was so surprised by Shūsaku's progress that he decided to have a personal contest with him. To be allowed to fight one's own *sensei* was a rare honour in those days when a master's pupils were numbered in their thousands. Nakanishi Chube'e's *dōjō* was selected as the venue, which was then one of the best-known *dōjō*s in Edo, evidence of how seriously Takai-*sensei* viewed the confrontation. It would have been no disgrace for Shūsaku to be beaten by Matashichirō, so he could put all his energy into it, win or lose. Shūsaku did not have confidence in a win, but realized that he had been given a golden opportunity to find out how good his technique really was. If he did win, of course, his name would become very famous.

It produced a duel that would have been remarkable at any time in samurai history. The *sensei* Takai Matashichirō had a strange technique. No matter whom he fought he would never let opponents touch his *shinai*. He

followed them pace for pace and at a good distance. At the moment of closing, when the swordsmen are a crucial distance apart, he controlled everything and everyone, and was best known for his 'soundless *kamae*'. The *kamae* was the situation when both swordsmen were eyeing each other up, ready to strike, and practically trying to stare each other out. Matashichirō always stood perfectly still, but also looked as if he had no intention of fighting. If the opponent tried to intimidate him Matashichirō gave no reaction whatsoever, making the opponent confused. Of course anyone who was impatient would be really frustrated, and his mind would begin to wander. When the opponent was at the end of his patience Matashichirō would suddenly strike. This unnerving period of waiting was what was called his 'soundless *kamae*'.

Up to then many people had fought with Matashichirō but nobody had been able to break his *kamae*. Shūsaku had witnessed it on several occasions, and knew very well that patience was the vital factor. So Shūsaku waited also and did not move, so that they looked like two people who had forgotten about fighting. Nakanishi Chube'e and his other pupils were watching, with nobody making any noise, feeling that if they blinked the fight would be over. Shūsaku continued to stand still, forcing himself not to start the fight because once he started, at that moment he would have a weak point and Matashichirō would take advantage of it. Matashichirō in fact showed a little genuine frustration, and an ordinary person waiting such a long time would have attacked, but Shūsaku still held his guard because he knew it was the only way he could possibly win.

After a seemingly endless wait even the *dōjō* master Nakanishi Chube'e became impatient and thought he would separate them, but suddenly they both moved simultaneously and the swords met. The famous soundless *kamae* was replaced by a clash of *shinai*, and almost immediately afterwards a loud crack! The floor of the *dōjō* had split beneath Shūsaku's feet! It was a very thick floor and such a thing had never happened before, evidence of the tremendous power of Shūsaku's *kiai*, the explosive energy of the swordsman released in a huge burst. The *dōjō* owner later cut out the piece of flooring and displayed it for the pupils to see, as an example of the supreme quality of swordsmanship.

The activity of Shūsaku's that caused the greatest stir was his showdown with one of the greatest schools in

CHIBA SHUSAKU/THE SWORD OF REVOLUTION

▲ **Cut down from behind** A sharp sword cuts into a fleeing samurai's head. (From the *Ehon Taikō-ki*)

Japan: the Maniwa Nen-ryū. He had just come to Takahashi, home of the Maniwa Nen-ryū, on his *musha-shugyō* pilgrimage. Shūsaku defeated a certain Koizumi in a contest, and this Koizumi was rumoured to be first among *bokutō* in the country. Because of this, hundreds of novice candidates had gathered to see Shūsaku, and all hoped to avenge Koizumi, while Shūsaku's own pupils naturally supported him. This was in 1822, and it was only the persuasive power of the chief magistrate of the locality that gradually settled it without a riot or major bloodshed.

The sword of revolution

Shūsaku eventually died in 1855, the last of the old-style *sensei* who could devote themselves entirely to the martial arts. Japan was changing rapidly, and the martial arts were changing with it. One year before Chiba Shūsaku died Japan had been shaken by the arrival off its coast of the American fleet commanded by Commodore Matthew Perry, which ended the two centuries of Japan's self-imposed isolation. It also brought into the open many dissenting voices who had been dissatisfied with the rule of the Tokugawa family, and who had their own ideas of how to face the new threat posed by foreign

nations. The supporters of the Shogun tended to co-operate with the Western nations, signing treaties and promoting trade. Their opponents believed that the Shogun's acquiescence in Western demands was a sign of weakness and a betrayal of traditional Japanese values, and saw a need to abolish the Shogunate, and restore that most Japanese of institutions: government by the divine Emperor. The rallying cry of these young activists was *Sonnō-jōi!* (Revere the Emperor and Expel the Barbarians!). The most extreme among this faction called themselves *shishi*, which means 'men of high purpose'. Hungry for revolutionary change within a Japanese context, they worked hard at improving their skills in the martial arts for the conflict they expected at any time. It is not surprising that they were joined by a new breed of 'lone warriors', eager to demonstrate their martial skills.

Their training was undertaken at the numerous *dōjō*s around the country, the *dōjō*s of Edo in particular providing an excellent opportunity for the young activists to meet, as much of their time was spent there when their *daimyō* was in Edo for his spell of residence required by the Shogun's law. As well as contests between individuals from two different *dōjō*s the later Tokugawa Period also witnessed some large-scale fencing matches between groups of rival schools. Probably the greatest contest of this sort took place in 1857, at the great meeting at the Kajibashi estate of the Tosa *han* in Edo. Through the generosity of the *daimyō* Yamauchi Yōdo, martial arts enthusiasts from many provinces gathered to compete and compare their skills. The referees and umpires were Saitō Yakurō of the Shintō Munen-ryū, Momonoi Shunzō of the Kyōshin meichi-ryū, and many others.

The programme for the contests lists many famous samurai of the day such as Sakamoto Ryōma from Tosa, and it is also very interesting to note that the vast majority of them were loyalist *shishi*, the young revolutionaries who within a few years were to overthrow the Shogunate and restore the Emperor, the decisive act in Japanese history that led to the modern Japanese state. The contest was indeed a gathering of famous swordsmen from all over Japan, but there is some evidence that martial arts were not the real reason for coming together, and that the sole reason for holding them was to provide cover for meetings between revolutionaries from distant provinces. Some of the contests may even have been

THE LAST OF THE SWORDSMEN

fabricated. It is very interesting to think that the *shishi* from different fiefs could not contact one another except in this way, and this adds a whole new dimension to the reasons for the popularity of the martial arts among these lower class samurai at the end of the Edo Period.

Not all of the young political activists, however, took such a cynical view of *bugei*. Many were genuinely devoted to *kenjutsu*, and in the case of one, at least, the skills he had developed by dedicated practice helped to save his life. This was the political activist from Tosa province called Sakamoto Ryōma, who was attacked one night by a *bakufu* murder squad. It is such a splendid tale of 'lone samurai' heroism that it is hard to believe that it actually took place in 1866, except for Sakamoto's use of a revolver to supplement his sword! He and his friend Miyoshi Shinzo were going to bed in an inn called the

▼ **Equipment for *kenjutsu* and *kendō*** A picture from Hokusai's sketchbooks showing various weapons and protective equipment.

Teradaya in Fushimi, near Kyōto, when they fancied they heard footsteps and the rattle of *bō*. At that point a maid raced upstairs and warned them that men with spears were coming to get them. The comrades pulled on their *hakama* trousers, seized their swords, and crouched down in a corner of the room to meet the attack. Twenty or so samurai were ascending the stairs and moving into an adjoining room. As they entered the room where the two *shishi* were concealed Sakamoto Ryōma brandished his revolver, at which the leaders withdrew, but others came against them and soon the fight grew fast and furious. One samurai leapt at Sakamoto out of the darkness and cut his left hand but, making good use of the six shots in his pistol and their sharp swords, the two managed to drive them temporarily out of the room. Sakamoto tried to reload his pistol, but the wound on his hand made it difficult, and all the while the enemy were to be heard outside. As he fumbled in the dark Sakamoto dropped the cartridge chamber and could not find it. His companion was all for rushing into the midst of the

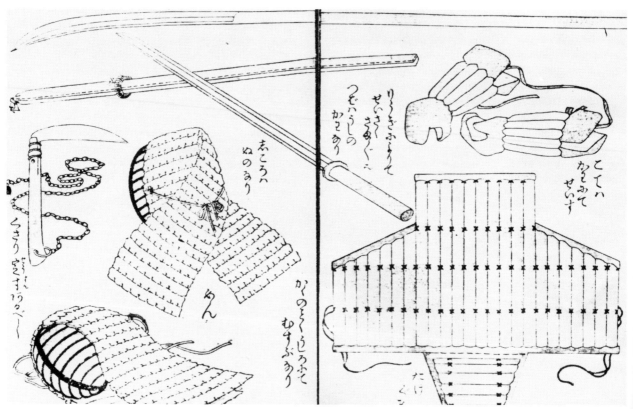

enemy in good old samurai style, but Sakamoto suggested they look for a way out. Fortunately the rear of the building was unguarded, so the two companions slipped down a ladder into the rear courtyard. As the courtyard was enclosed there was no direct way out except through one of the buildings that surrounded it. All the shutters of the house next to them were locked, so the only way of escape was literally to bash their way through the entire house. This they proceeded to do with gusto. After smashing through the outer wooden shutters they found themselves in a bedroom, occupied by several rather startled inhabitants. Believing that the shortest distance between two points was a straight line, the two *shishi* drew their swords and headed for the open street, cutting through each *shōji* (sliding screen window), as they came to it. The house proved to be rather large, so by the time they had made it out into the street Sakamoto and his comrade had cut and kicked their way through several rooms, leaving a series of irregular holes behind them.

The swordsman assassins

The two *shishi* eventually escaped, but many of their contemporaries on both sides of the political divide fell prey to the assassin's sword or bullet during the reign of terror that marred the years of change. Few of these acts of terrorism are admirable in any way. There is little 'martial arts' skill involved in murdering a politician or a police spy, particularly when it is accompanied by the anachronistic and sickening act of displaying his head. The years that saw the niceties of *dōjō* behaviour, with old *sensei* behaving as if they were living in the sixteenth century, gave way to a background of needless violence, as the young samurai divided into two armed camps:

▼ **An assassination** The victim is caught off guard, and handicapped by wearing the very long *naga-bakama*, the form of trousers worn to Court, that extended past the feet, which made rapid movement impossible. (From the *Ehon Taikō-ki*)

those who supported the continuation of the Shogun and his policy of opening up Japan to the West, and the others, the *shishi*, who saw in the Emperor a way of uniting the country and expelling the barbarians. To balance the picture presented by the examples of Chiba Shūsaku, Otani Nobutomo, and the exciting romance of Sakamoto's escape, let us spend some time examing the dark side of martial prowess in later Tokugawa Japan.

In 1862, a leading *bakufu* supporter, Shimada Sakon, was killed by an assassin. His head was exposed at Shijōgawara, to the astonishment of the Kyōto people. This was to be known as the 'first instalment of *tenchū* (heavenly punishment), in Kyōto, and the assassins made it clear that they had killed him as a reaction against the *bakufu* authority. Later that year Homma Seiichirō was murdered, and his bloody head was similarly exposed at Shijō, another victim of *tenchū*. In the following year Anegakōji Kintomo was attacked by three assassins who ran along the old imperial palace wall as he was leaving the gate. His companion Yoshimura Ukyō fought hard but in vain, and, seriously wounded, he was carried to his residence and there died. The assassins of these men were not ordinarily thought of as terrorists, simply passionate young men who felt they had to kill recklessly and with blind devotion. One distinctive feature of the assassins was that they were at the end of their youth, aged between 25 and 30, and of the lower samurai rank. There was little approval of their acts, and many of their political sympathizers saw them as a hindrance to the revolution, with assassination as a cowardly and most evil way of justifying their position.

As an example of these assassins we may mention the three men Kawakami Gensei, Tanaka Shinbe'e and Okada Izō. Kawakami was the second son of a low-ranking samurai of the Higo *han*, and was adopted into the underlying Kawakami family, served as a cleaning boy, and at puberty joined the loyalist party. In 1862 he became a member of the Imperial Court guard. Later he became deeply involved with the *shishi* of Chōshū, and in 1864 he murdered a student of Western learning called Sakuma Shōzan in Kyōto. Genzai also became displeased with the new Meiji Government, and was sentenced to death because of his anti-government movement. The public called him 'Hitokiri Genzai' ('Genzai the killer'). Tanaka was the son of a sea captain, and became a Satsuma samurai by the assistance of the wealthy merchants. He mixed with *shishi* of many provinces on their journeys to Kyōto, and was transformed into one of the bad elements of the radicals. Tanaka was said to be involved in the assassinations of Shimada Sakon, Ukyō Omokuni and Homma Seiichirō, and he eventually took the title of '*ansatsu taichō*' (the captain of assassins). He was finally arrested as the criminal assassin of a girl called Komichi. When he was examined all the evidence pointed towards him, but at that moment he ended his life by *seppuku* with his own sword. Okada was an underling of the Tsuchiya and set out for the capital to use his assassin's sword. He was involved in the killing of Homma Seiichiro and acquired the title of 'Hitokiri Izō', but at the downfall of the Tsuchiya Imperialist party he was arrested, and in 1865 he was sentenced to be beheaded.

The noble swordsmen

Whatever prowess these men may have had in *bugei*, there is nothing to admire in such terrorist acts, but fortunately for the future of Japan an involvement by martial artists in politics did not necessarily mean revolution and assassination, and many of the top swordsmen served their country, and its reconstruction, in peaceful ways. Some behaved as nobly as any old *sensei*, combining public service with a keen appreciation of the place of the martial arts in the emerging state of Japan. Two of the best examples are Sakakibara Kenkichi and Takahashi Deishū. The Sakakibara family were Shogun's vassals over several generations, and Kenkichi was born in 1830. At the age of thirteen he became a pupil of Otani Nobutomo's Jikishinkage-ryū and studied *kenjutsu*, eventually becoming his best student. As the family were poor they thought they would have to defer his receipt of a *menkyo* (licence to teach), but the master Nobutomo, realizing this, granted it free of charge. In 1856 he was appointed on the recommendation of Nobutomo to the post of professor at the Kobushu, a newly formed office of the Shogunate to take charge of training, including Western-style army organization and gunnery. There was to be reform in military organization, with a regular army of three divisions: footsoldiers, cavalry, and artillery. As a result of this involvement Sakakibara Kenkichi became a close confidant of the Shogun Iemochi and served as his bodyguard.

Traditional martial arts were not forgotten, however, and Kenkichi had a famous contest with one of his

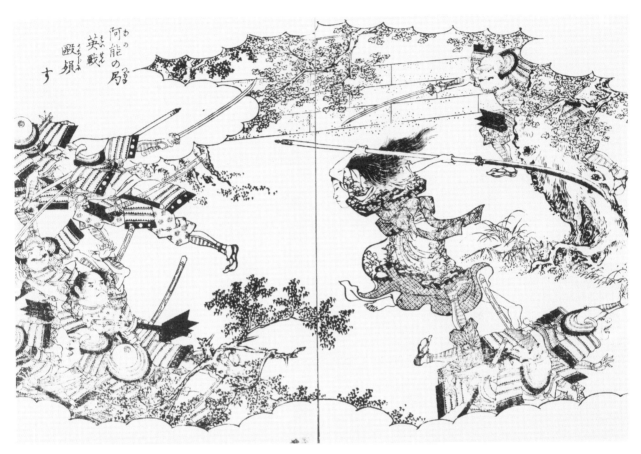

▲ **Girl with *naginata*** The *naginata* developed from a fierce polearm to a weapon regarded as suitable for women to exercise with. In this picture from the *Ehon Taikō-ki* a woman uses it for its original purpose.

contemporaries, Takahashi Deishū. Deishū had been born in 1835, and was thus five years younger than Kenkichi. In 1856 he was chosen as professor of *yari-jutsu* at the Kobushu. In this connection, at this time, among the twelve names of professors of *yari-jutsu*, there were nine from the famous Hōzō-In-ryū, whose ancestor had almost beaten Miyamoto Musashi. When he became a master of *yari-jutsu* Deishū had had a famous contest with a certain Ii Kanehira. Kanehira had over thirty years' experience, and his spear work was strong. His speciality was to tease his opponent with his spear, holding him firmly at a distance, and then, seizing the moment, he would make a wide slash and sweep the

opponent's legs away from under him with a cut called *ashi-guruma*. This technique had won him many contests. The experience had stood Deishū in good stead, and he was now said to be the best in Japan at spear techniques.

The contest between Kenkichi and Deishū was bound to be an unusual one, as it was to match a sword against a spear. As both men were in the favour of the Shogun Iemochi it was decided that the contest should be held in his presence, an immense honour, and one that was almost unique since the days of Yagyū Munenori. The contest took place in 1860 amid great ceremony, and both men appear to have risen to the occasion. Kenkichi began by lifting his sword to the *jōdan* position, and taunting Deishū into thrusting at an apparently un-guarded point. Deishū was cautious, holding his spear out before him, and instead of aiming at Kenkichi's chest drove a blow at his face. Kenkichi dodged, and landed several blows with his *shinai* on Deishū's spear. From then on the contest became fast and furious as each scored points off the other. However, Deishū had the advantage of youth over the older Kenkichi, and after much contact gained an advantage, at which point the Shogun, well satisfied, stopped the two men from fighting further.

This brilliant display of martial arts was probably the last friendly encounter with weapons that any Shogun was to witness. When the Tokugawa administration collapsed, and the Tokugawa family moved to Suruga, the samurai who had supported him were split up. Sakakibara Kenkichi was employed as a prison guard at the Metropolitan Police Headquarters. These were dark days for martial artists. The samurai were abolished as a class, sword-wearing was banned to all except the armed forces, and the anachronistic rebellions which I shall describe at the end of this chapter cast a shadow over the noble traditions of the old *sensei*.

Sakakibara Kenkichi was one of the few who tried to raise their popularity by making an entertainment of a *kenjutsu* match, but even this has an air of desperation about it, of trying to revive something that was virtually dead. The most bizarre example of this was a 'sideshow' he put on in 1889 called *kabuto-wari* (helmet breaking), a form of martial arts entertainment that makes one wince to think about it. The object of the contest was to use swords to cut through a helmet, an exercise that can have done no good either to helmet or to sword. The helmet used was a Myōchin-forged, pear-shaped design of foreign steel, in other words, a masterpiece by the leading school of armour-makers in Japan. Swordsmen called Itsumi Sōsuke and Ueda Uma-no-jō and others were among the great names that competed, but although the helmet was scarred it could not be cut into. Then Kenkichi had a try. He used a *dōtamune* stroke, and swung it at the brow, making a splendid three-and-a-half-inch cut in it. He was well satisfied at this display of skill, and we are told, his reputation grew. Fortunately for the future antique trade no more such contests are on record, and the development of the martial arts turned more in the direction of *budō* and the sports-orientated forms we are used to today. In 1895 Kenkichi died, and was compared to the finest swordsmen who have ever lived, as may be his former rival Takahashi Deishū, who served as land registrar under the Meiji Government, and outlived every other contemporary swordsman, to die peacefully in 1903.

Yamaoka Tesshū

We must also mention the name of Yamaoka Tesshū, another late master, whose career includes many elements of the great *sensei* in a modern context. He was born in 1836, and trained in the Hokushin Ittō-ryū under Chiba Shūsaku. He was devoted to *kenjutsu*, and at the age of twenty-seven he challenged to a match Asari Matashichirō, the current master of the Ittō-ryū, whom he failed to beat. This failure made him devote himself to training in swordsmanship and Zen Buddhism, with the aim of meeting Asari Matashichirō again one day. His training was interrupted by the Restoration wars when he served in the Shogun's guard. His most worthwhile contribution to the war was made not by fighting, proving that the discipline of the swordsman could have very real value in a peaceful context. Following the defeat of the Shogun's army at Toba-Fushimi near Kyōto, the Shogun withdrew to Edo, pursued by the Imperial army. Yamaoka Tesshū was entrusted with a vital mission. He was to go and meet the commander of the Imperial army half-way and negotiate a settlement so that Edo would not be attacked. This he succeeded in doing, thereby undoubtedly saving many innocent lives.

In 1880, with Japan at peace, Yamaoka Tesshū finally got a chance to meet Asari Matashichirō again after a lapse of seventeen years. They made a challenge, an almost unique arrangement for two old masters at this late date, and faced each other across the *dōjō* floor, each with his *shinai* at the ready. But Asari Matashichirō noticed the change that had taken place in the younger man over the passing of time. He recognized the new quality in his opponent, his new confidence and his obvious spiritual insight, so, in a chivalrous gesture that would not have been out of place in the age of Kamiizumi Nobutsuna, instead of fighting with him he immediately conferred upon him the *menkyo-kaiden* of the Ittō-ryū. Yamaoka Tesshū died in 1888, and five thousand people from among the grateful citizens of Edo watched his funeral procession pass the Imperial Palace. Even Emperor Meiji, it was said, watched the cortege from a window.

The last lone samurai

It would be wrong to conclude this chapter with anyone other than the reactionaries of the Meiji Period whose rebellions scarred the face of Meiji Japan, but whose use

YAMAOKA TESSHU/THE LAST LONE SAMURAI

▲ **The lone samurai** This lone samurai is not a *rōnin*, but in the service of a *daimyō*, as shown by the *mon* (badge) on his formal clothes.

sentiments by a petition presented by a Kyūshū samurai to the government in protest against the act. His comments make the reaction to a ban on swords sound somewhat like the opposition to gun control in the USA, but on a much more spiritual level. The bearing of swords, like guns, is seen as a civil right and a valuable safeguard for law and order. The novelist Yukio Mishima quotes it in his novel *Homba* (Runaway Horses), and its reference to ancient times provides an interesting link with the early swords and swordbearers of Japan (my translation):

'In my view the bearing of swords is a custom that characterized our land even in the ancient era of the gods and Emperor Jimmu. It is closely bound up with the origins of our country, it enhances the dignity of the imperial throne, solemnizes the rites of our gods, banishes the spirits of evil, and puts down disorders. The sword, therefore, not only maintains the tranquility of the nation but also guards the safety of the individual citizen. Indeed the one thing essential to this martial nation that reveres the gods, the one thing that can never be set aside even for one moment, is the sword. How then could those upon whom is laid the burden of fashioning and executing a national policy that honours the gods and strengthens our land be so forgetful of the sword?'

of *bugei*, often in preference to western weaponry, makes their anachronistic attempts memorable. One of the main spurs to action by these groups was the government's ban on the wearing of swords to all but the armed forces. This was doubly insulting to the samurai class, because the new army had been formed by conscription from among all classes. The probable reaction to such a ban was anticipated by Lord Redesdale in his *Tales of Old Japan*: 'The statesman who shall enact a law forbidding the carrying of this deadly weapon will indeed have deserved well of his country; but it will be a difficult task to undertake, and a dangerous one. I would not give much for that man's life. The hand of every swashbuckler in the country would be against him.'

Lord Redesdale's lavish prose was in fact echoed in its

This sentiment was widely echoed, and one of the most dramatic reactions was a rebellion that occurred in the town of Kumamoto, where two hundred former samurai, enraged at what they saw as the government's abandonment of Japanese traditions for Western decadence, formed a league which they called the *kami-kaze*, thus identifying themselves with the tempest that sank the Mongol fleet in the thirteenth century. They had very extreme views, and bizarre ways of expressing them. For instance, they regarded all Western introductions, such as telegraph wires, as defilements of their sacred lands, and felt themselves obliged to walk under wires with their heads covered by white paper fans. If they so much as glimpsed someone wearing Western clothes they would purify themselves by scattering salt.

In an attempt to act unsullied by the decadent Western technology they refused to carry guns or other Western weapons, and launched themselves in an attack on the Imperial garrison using only swords. They were mown down by the defenders' firepower, and committed suicide

THE LAST OF THE SWORDSMEN

THE LAST LONE SAMURAI

to a man. Mishima tries to explain their actions in *Homba*:

'. . . what the men of the League had been willing to risk by renouncing their use of firearms had clarified their intent. Divine aid was to be theirs, and their very purpose was to challenge the Western arms hateful to the gods, by swords alone. Western civilization would as time went by search out weapons still more terrible and would direct them at Japan . . . To rise to the combat bearing only the sword, to be willing to risk even more crushing defeat, in this way could the fervent aspirations of each man of the League take expression. Here was the essence of the gallant Yamato spirit.'

◄ **Death of a samurai** A dramatic print by Yoshitoshi, which sums up the defiant end of the lone samurai when faced with modern weapons. (Courtesy of the Oranda-jin Gallery, the Netherlands)

The fighters of the better-known Satsuma Rebellion of 1877 did not scorn Western-style weapons. They still claimed the 'Yamato spirit', and saw themselves as vastly superior to the 'conscripted peasants' of the newly formed Imperial army in training, motivation, and above all in the sincerity of their cause. This demonstration of *makoto* led to probably the last sword combat in Japan when the Satsuma rebels attacked Kumamoto castle. Both sides were desperately short of ammunition, and samurai swords were used by both armies in the fierce hand-to-hand fighting which resulted when the rebels scaled the walls. Their leader Saigō Takamori also died dramatically, committing suicide when he was pursued and finally beaten. Like Prince Yamato, this final example of the lone samurai died a lonely death in the true spirit of the lone warrior.

▼ **The old sensei** A photograph showing a master of the Maniwa Nen-ryū in action with wooden weapons.

13.

The Eternal Lone Samurai

The past hundred years have seen some remarkable changes in the views which the Japanese, and the rest of the world, have held about the figure of the samurai warrior. Just as the ancient *bugei* have been virtually replaced by modern *budō*, so has the image of the samurai changed in a radical way. In this chapter I intend to explore the ways in which not one, but a series of images have been created, expanded and demolished depending upon the circumstances of the time.

The early years of modern Japan saw an extraordinary paradox in its view of the samurai. On the one hand there was the abolition of the samurai as a class, which was both symbolized and realized by the ban on wearing swords by anyone except members of the newly formed conscript army. This was accompanied by a certain playing down of the samurai ethos in favour of what were perceived as the military needs of a modern nation, as illustrated in the last chapter by the attempts of Sakakibara Kenkichi to revive interest through popular entertainment. Yet at the same time as the class was abolished as an actual entity we also see the beginning of a glorification of the samurai as a myth. It is a myth which supported Japan during its modernization, served the ultra-nationalist politics of the 1930s, and has endured through film and television to the present day.

The glorification of Kusunoki

One of the earliest illustrations of the samurai myth is the development of the cult of Kusunoki Masashige, which puts the whole of the samurai image into sharp focus. The Kusunoki Masashige of myth represents the samurai as being the ideal of Japanese behaviour. The historical Masashige was of course the commander whose exploits defending the castles of Akasaka and Chihaya were discussed in Chapter Three. These activities were gallant enough, but the most important part of the Kusunoki legend, however, concerns his death in 1336 at the Battle of Minatogawa, the circumstances of which made him the perfect samurai hero.

The background to the battle is as follows. Having restored Emperor Go-Daigo to his throne the Kusunoki managed to chase away their rivals of the Ashikaga clan until they left the mainland of Honshū for Kyūshū. But by 1336 the Ashikaga had fought back and were approaching Kyōto along the coast of the Inland Sea.

THE GLORIFICATION OF KUSUNOKI

▲ **Kusunoki Masashige** The Meiji Restoration turned Kusunoki Masashige from a samurai hero into the perfect example of loyal behaviour.

Kusunoki's ally Nitta Yoshisada had set up camp where the estuary of the Minato river joins the sea. (This is now within the city of Kobe.) Emperor Go-Daigo ordered Kusunoki Masashige to join Nitta and make a stand against the enemy, but Masashige advised the Emperor that they would be better advised to withdraw to the mountains and fight a guerrilla campaign once again. This was the type of warfare that had served them so well in the past and had enabled Go-Daigo to achieve his present position. It was a wise judgement of the military situation, but Go-Daigo, unwilling to become a fugitive again, refused, insisting that the loyalist forces could easily overwhelm the Ashikaga. As the Emperor had made up his mind there was nothing Kusunoki Masashige could do other than to accept the will of his sovereign, so he set out for Minatogawa to what he knew would be a certain defeat. After many hours of fierce fighting he and his brother committed *hara-kiri* and entered the pantheon of Japanese heroes in a way in which their dogged but successful guerrilla campaigns could never have achieved for them.

These are the bare bones of the Kusunoki legend, which later years were to flesh into the perfect example of the lone samurai, dying heroically against enormous odds, fighting bravely even though he knows the cause is hopeless. Kusunoki Masashige is therefore honoured twice, once for being loyal to the Emperor, and secondly for being loyal to his *makoto*, the vital concept of sincerity to the calling of a samurai. It is worth noting at this stage that the Kusunoki legend had to wait at least two and a half centuries after his death before it could really get going. The much maligned Ashikaga dynasty, of whom Ashikaga Takauji, victor of Minatogawa, became the first Shogun in 1338, reigned for nearly as long as the later Tokugawa. For Masashige to become a hero Takauji had to become a villain, and it is quite clear that for the first two centuries of Ashikaga rule the positions were totally reversed, with the Kusunoki regarded as opportunistic troublemakers and a hindrance to the creation of the benevolent rule of the Ashikaga. But in 1563 things started to change, and Kusunoki Masashige was accorded a posthumous pardon. The Ashikaga Shogunate was by then crumbling, and Masashige provided an alternative hero, boosted by the growing popularity of the *Taiheiki*, which recounts his exploits in much glowing detail.

THE ETERNAL LONE SAMURAI

During the Tokugawa Period several influential Confucian scholars saw in Kusunoki Masashige the perfect illustration of the twin virtues of *kō* (filial piety) and *chū* (loyalty) which were to play such a part in the formulation of *bushidō*. As to his loyalty, Rai Sannyō (1780–1832) saw him as the most glorious example of all, giving up his life even when the cause he was fighting for was at its weakest. The doctrine of filial piety also receives its finest blessing with the Kusunoki family in the famous story of Masashige's parting with his son before going off to Minatogawa. The young Masatsura, then aged ten, accompanied his father as far as the town of Sakurai, where Masashige bade him farewell, handing on to him the sword he had received from the Emperor Go-Daigo, and charging him with continuing the fight after his father was dead. This Masatsura was to do to the letter, and eventually met his own sincere and heroic death at the Battle of Shijo-Nawate in 1348.

The parting of father and son at Sakurai formed the theme of a patriotic song of the Meiji Period. Entitled *Aoba Shigareru Sakurai no,* which is the first line of the first verse, beginning, 'Evening draws nigh at Sakurai's leafy ford . . . ', it goes on to tell of the parting, and was taught in all Japanese elementary schools before the Second World War. Such was the popularity of the Kusunoki family during those turbulent years.

The early Meiji government of course, took one particular aspect of the Kusunoki legend to its heart, that he had been fighting for the Emperor. No other hero in samurai history offers this in any way. The earlier and abortive rebellion by Go-Toba seems to have inspired no such sacrifice, and no hero of note on the loyalist side. The great fighters of the Sengoku Period fought for their *daimyō,* not for the Emperor. They may have had the same honourable code of conduct, and showed the same virtues of *makoto,* loyalty and obedience, enshrined in the examples of *bushidō,* but Kusunoki Masashige alone displays all the *bushidō* virtues of loyalty in return for benevolence on behalf of the Emperor. The Meiji Restoration was an imperial restoration which succeeded, and Kusunoki Masashige provided its ideal hero, combining the perfect focus of behaviour with the perfect direction for that behaviour. So, over five hundred years after his death he was raised to the 'Junior First Rank' of the imperial court, and a statue was erected outside the imperial palace in Tōkyō. To honour him at the spot where he fell the Minatogawa Shrine was founded in Kobe. It was burned down during the war but has since been rebuilt, and houses a fascinating museum.

The adulation of Masashige reached its height during the ultra-nationalist 1930s, when every school history book presented him as the most noble samurai in Japanese history, and in 1945 the Kusunoki story inspired the desperate and wasteful suicide attacks, including the *kami-kaze* suicide pilots. On the first mission by the pilots of *Oka* bombers (the one-man suicide bombs carried close to their target under the belly of a bomber), the squadron pennant bore the characters *HI RI HO KEN TEN,* which was an abbreviation of a famous saying attributed to Kusunoki Masashige referring to the triumph of truth (*ri*) over wrong (*hi*), and the triumph of heaven (*ten*) over all. The leader of the raid, Lieutenant-Commander Nonaka, said as he climbed into his aircraft, 'This is my Minatogawa.' Other attack squadrons had historical connections in the names they chose. Phrases referring to early names for Japan, such as *Yamato,* were popular but Kusunoki Masashige appears to be the only historical figure to whom allusion is made, such as in the use of the term *kikusui* ('chrysanthemum on the water' — the Kusunoki family *mon* or badge) for several suicide operations, proof that he was held in unique esteem.

Worship of Masashige of course suffered an enormous reverse with the end of the war and the occupation, and I was given an unusual illustration of this in 1986 when I was taken by two friends to visit the site of the Battle of Shijo-Nawate. Shijo-Nawate was the battle in 1348 at which Masashige's son Masatsura was defeated, and has become quite well-known in the West because it is illustrated in a much-reproduced print by Kuniyoshi entitled 'The last stand of the Kusunoki clan at the Battle of Shijo-Nawate'. The Shijo-Nawate shrine is on a hill overlooking the actual battle site which is half a mile away. It is now almost entirely built-up, but we drove down to it for no other good reason than that one of my companions was a former pupil of Shijo-Nawate High School. Having looked at her old school, our other friend, who is very interested in local history, took us a few hundred yards further down the road to visit Masatsura's grave, which is marked by a shrine fence and a camphor tree (*kusuno-ki* means camphor tree). What was extraordinary about this visit was to be told by our companion that she had attended the High School for several years, and yet had never been told, and did not know, that

▲ **The last poem of Kusunoki Masatsura** Before departing for the Battle of Shijo-Nawate, in which he was to die in a manner similar to that of his father, Kusunoki Masatsura wrote a farewell poem on the door of the Nyoirin-ji in Yoshino.

almost next door was the grave of a man who was regarded as one of her country's greatest heroes. Fifty years earlier, I am sure, all the pupils of the locality would have had to make official visits to revere the example of the Kusunoki family. In the 1960s it was almost as if the place, and the person, did not exist.

Of ants and men

If the image of the lone samurai, as personified most forcefully by Kusunoki Masashige, was the figure which inspired the Japanese fighting man of the Second World War, to what extent did this image come across to those fighting against him? Louis Allen, in his history of the Burma Campaign, devotes several pages to a discussion of how the Allies and the Japanese saw one another. He refers specifically to a discussion held in 1948 between a group of British diplomats and generals. The generals (Slim and Percival) commented particularly upon the bravery of the Japanese, and disagreed that Japanese society was essentially a group-led one in which the individual shirked responsibility and initiative. Slim saw Japanese courage as an individual rather than a group characteristic, and pointed out that he would fight on alone and not surrender.

One could well counter this argument by pointing out that the main reason why they fought on so desperately was that they had been ordered to do so. To surrender was quite unthinkable. To be captured and returned to Japan was a prospect so disgraceful that it was commonly thought that one was better off dead. There are innumerable examples to illustrate this, all of which, of course, fit in perfectly with the *bushidō* ideals of filial piety (obeying orders unquestioningly) and loyalty. Yet the response to this has still to be an individual one, as Kōsaka Danjō appreciated in his comments in the *Kōyō Gunkan*, and the individual bravery of Japanese soldiers was well recognized by the Allies. Slim, however, went on to use a notorious metaphor, when he compared the Japanese troops to soldier ants, 'the most formidable fighting insect in history'. This dehumanizing comparison was no doubt one often entertained by the ordinary British soldier, as the Japanese swarmed down in their hundreds upon him. But this image contradicts another popular wartime misconception about the Japanese soldier, that he was somehow superhuman rather than less than human. Many regarded the Japanese as natural jungle fighters, which they were not, having had less experience of jungles than had the British, but it still shows the difficulty of comprehending an enemy when there is such a gulf of language, culture and distance. As a schoolboy in the 1950s I can recall both images coming to me as received wisdom from different sources, reinforced many times over by films, comics and the reminiscences of ex-servicemen.

▼ **The site of the Battle of Shijo-Nawate** The site of the 'last stand' of the Kusunoki family is marked by this shrine to Masatsura. Note the enormous camphor tree and the Kusunoki *mon* on the gates.

The unity of bushidō

The image of the lone, sacrificial warrior may have been kept from the students of Shijo-Nawate High School as Japan recovered from the war and began her economic miracle, but it did not fail to attract the attentions of others. In an article entitled 'Death and Honour in Japan' Louis Allen examines the motivation of certain Japanese extremists who have come to prominence in the last twenty years. His discovery is that there is a unifying creed linking extremists and terrorists at both ends of the political spectrum. What motivates them most of all are not the ideologies of the groups they support (such as the PLO), but certain models from Japanese history, and above all the concept of *makoto* (sincerity), the virtue recommended above all others by Torii Mototada to his son prior to his death at Fushimi castle in 1600. Allen quotes Yukio Mishima, the author who committed suicide in 1970, who wrote about the things he had in common with left-wing student groups. Although they believed in the opposite political ideals from Mishima, they had in common a rigorous ideology, a taste for physical violence, and believed passionately in *makoto*, the very ideal that inspired Kusunoki Masashige in his sincere fidelity to the imperial cause.

His most interesting analysis is of Kozo Okamoto of the Japanese 'Red Army'. Okamoto was one of three terrorists who landed at Lod airport in May 1972 and

THE UNITY OF BUSHIDO

sprayed the customs hall with bullets and grenades, killing scores of people until they themselves were gunned down or captured. Okamoto survived and was imprisoned. His writings were smuggled out of prison, and give a strange insight into his motivation. What comes over very clearly is that Okamoto's most cherished ideas are not derived from left-wing politics but from the myths and traditions of the Japanese warrior. They reflect the feeling for the inevitability of suicide on behalf of an ideal, and the importance of the example set by historical figures. Okamoto's writings also show a bizarre side in the traditional love which the samurai had for the beauties of nature. In Allen's words, describing

---

▼ *Jū-jutsu* A page from the Hokusai sketchbooks showing various *jū-jutsu* techniques.

the terrorists training in Lebanon, they '. . . would finish their after-dinner grenade-throwing with a session of moon-viewing', and reflect on the transient nature of the life of the butterfly.

Okamoto was born in Kumamoto, in Kyūshū, and one incident that was very much in his mind was the revolt in 1876 by the *kami-kaze* league, which took place in Kumamoto. He was also much in sympathy with Wang Yang Ming Confucianism which taught that words had always to be accompanied by actions, that knowing without acting meant that one did not know, a powerful ideology that fanned the fervour of the *shishi* of the later Tokugawa Period. While on his flight to Lod to carry out the massacre Okamoto reflected on the acceptance of suicide by his predecessors in the *kami-kaze* league. Did they eat before committing suicide, he asked himself? His mind apparently also went to a story told about Admiral Togo who commanded the Japanese fleet against the Russians in 1905. Before the crucial battle of the Sea of Japan the Admiral was apparently so relaxed that his testicles hung loosely, a proof of courage that Okamoto was disappointed to find was not reflected in his own anatomy. (He apparently checked in the lavatory in the aeroplane). The point is that here an international terrorist is expressing his feelings in a totally Japanese framework, in a way which he had in common with his political enemies. Okamoto, like Mishima, followed the self-destructive path of *makoto*, just as so many had before him.

The actions of the 'Red Army', and the suicide of Mishima, represent the dark side of the myth of the lone samurai. The lighter side has come through film, television and literature. The wandering heroes of *Seven Samurai* brought the image of the samurai warrior to millions round the globe. Like *geisha* and cherry blossoms, the samurai of Kurosawa's films have become a Japanese cliché, but the ethos of the lone warrior has never been better portrayed either before or since. Subsequent productions such as *Sanjuro* and *Yōjimbō* have reinforced the genre, while television and video have made them available to a wider audience. A further vehicle for popularizing the lone samurai idea is the comic book, though until recently this was confined to Japan. The most successful productions in this category are the adventures of Itto Ogami, the 'Lone Wolf', who wanders the countryside accompanied by his infant son. Ogami is the archetype of the lone samurai. He uses real swords

THE SPIRIT OF THE LONE SAMURAI

◄ **Toshiro Mifune** Toshiro Mifune in one of his most celebrated roles as the wandering samurai in *Sanjurō*.

indiscriminately, is always victorious, and follows an obsessive quest resulting from his banishment from the Shogun's service through the machinations of the Yagyū family. 'Lone Wolf' has spawned a television series in Japan, and is to the younger generation what Toshiro Mifune's roles were to the previous one.

The spirit of the lone samurai

Japan is once again going through a period of change, and as the country faces the future with the new Emperor it is appropriate to reflect on the reality and the value of these samurai ideals today. Here again we find a paradox. In many popular comics the activities of samurai are depicted with a graphic violence that would never be acceptable in this country, yet it is well-recognized that Japanese streets are the safest to walk in after dark. This is the public face of things, but it is well to recognize that the forces of extremism can lurk very close to the surface. Right-wing groups in Japan are pressing for a re-writing of school history text books, so that incidents like the Rape of Nanking in 1938 can be played down, or even denied. The teachers' unions have opposed this move, which has put them into direct opposition to some small but very dangerous nationalist groups. Union meetings have been attacked, and a union leader was recently held hostage with the blade of a samurai sword against his throat, a sickening footnote to samurai history.

Throughout Japanese history the death-defying, and often death-seeking lone samurai has so frequently provided what he sees as the moral renewal for the nation. When reason falters, *makoto* rushes to fill the moral vacuum. But must the spirit of loyalty, of action and of sincerity only find its expression in terms of destructive violence? Must every reaction to Western values and nihilism be expressed in this way? Perhaps there is hope. Every old battlefield in Japan contains a shrine, and at each of the shrines I have managed to visit I have discovered that someone has erected a simple short pillar with, in Japanese and English, the words, 'May peace prevail through the world.' It reminds every visitor, I hope, that the study of war is the study of man's folly. On the individual level, too, there is folly even among the virtues of sincerity, loyalty and benevolence.

As Japan begins a new era we can only pray that these virtues which have proved so destructive in the past can be harnessed for peaceful ends, and the lone samurai cease to be a vehicle of destruction. The modern development of the martial arts provides one possible vehicle whereby the spirit of the lone samurai can provide a link with the past, and become a positive force, enriching the health and the culture of Japanese youth, and providing a secure bridge between East and West. If through martial arts, and also via shared entertainment within sensible limits of taste, the lone warrior can become a harmonizing and creative source, there is hope for the world, and peace may prevail.

▲ **Early morning** *kata* A present-day *bugei* practitioner is caught by the author's camera as he practises *kata* early one morning in the forests of Yamanashi.

Bibliography

Primary sources are shown as reference to the most modern edition of the work, or is cross-referenced to a modern 'compilation' volume containing it. Translations into English of such works are listed under the name of the translator.

Allen, Louis. *Burma, The Longest War*. London, 1984
— 'Death and Honour in Japan', in *The Listener*, 24 June 1976
Bottomley l, and Hopson, J. *Arms and Armour of the Samurai*. London, 1988
Brownlee, John. 'The *Shōkyū* War and the political rise of the Warriors', in *Monumenta Nipponica*, vol. 24, nos. 1–2
Butler, Kenneth. 'The *Heike Monogatari* and the Japanese Warrior Ethic', in *Harvard Journal of Asian Studies*, vol. 29
Daidōji, Yuzan. *Budō Shōshinshū*. Tokyo, 1941
Harris, Victor. The Book of Five Rings, *Gorinshō*, by Miyamoto Musashi, London, 1974
Hawley, Willis. *Introduction to Japanese Swords*. Los Angeles, 1973
Hearn, Lafcadio. *Japan: An Interpretation*. Rutland Vt., 1955
Imamura, Yoshio. *Nihon Budō Zenshū*. Tokyo, 1962
Ise, Sadatake. *Gunyōki*. Edo, 1843
Jansen, Marius. *Sakamoto Ryōma and the Meiji Restoration*. Stanford, 1971
Kammer, Reinhard. The Way of the Sword, the *Tengu Geijutsu-ron* of Chozan Shissai. London, 1978
Kellogg, Edward. Selective Translation of *Hōgen Monogatari* in Transactions of the Asiatic Society of Japan, 45 1917
Kofujita, Toshisada. *Ittōsai Sensei Kenposhō* in Saigusa et. al., 1957
Kōsaka, Danjō. *Kōyō Gunkan* in *Sengoku Shiryō soshō*, vols. 3–5, Tokyo, 1965
Knutsen, Roald M. *Japanese Polearms*. London, 1963
Lindsay, K and Kano, J. 'Jiu-jutsu', in Transactions of the Asiatic Society of Japan, 16 1889
McCullough, William. '*Shōkyū-ki* – An Account of the *Shōkyū* War of 1221', in *Monumenta Nipponica*, vol. 19, 1–2
— 'The *Azuma-kagami* account of the *Shōkyū* War' in *Monumenta Nipponica*, vol. 23, 1–2
Morris, Ivan. *The Nobility of Failure*. London, 1975
Okubo, Tadataka. *Mikawa Monogatari*. Tokyo, 1974

Ono, Yasumaro, et. al. *Kojiki* in *Nihon Koten Zenshō*, vol. 1, Tokyo, 1962
Sadler, A.L. '*Heike Monogatari*', in Transactions of the Asiatic Society of Japan, Yokohama, 1911, 1913
Saigusa, Hiroto and Miyagawa, Akira. *Nihon Tetsugaki Shisō Zenshū*, vol. 15, Tokyo, 1957
Satō, Kan'ichi. *Nihon no tōken*. Tokyo, 1963
Takuan, Sōhō. '*Fūdochi shinmyōroku*', in Saigusa et. al., 1957
Toneri, Shinno et. al. *Nihon Shōki* in *Shintei Zōhō Kokushi Taikei*, vol. 1, Tokyo, 1951
Tsukahara, Bokuden. *Bokuden Ikun-sho* in Imamura, 1966
Turnbull, Stephen. *The Samurai – A Military History*. London, 1977, 1988
— *Samurai Armies, 1550–1615*. London, 1979
— *Warlords of Japan*. London, 1979
— *The Book of the Samurai*. London, 1982
— *Samurai Warriors*. London, 1987
— *Battles of the Samurai*. London, 1987
— *Samurai Warlords – The Book of the Daimyō*. London, 1989
— *The Ninja* (in preparation)
Watatani, Kiyoshi. *Nihon kengō hyakusen*. Tokyo, 1971
— *Bugei ryūha hyakusen*. Tokyo, 1972
Wilson, William R. 'The Way of the Bow and Arrow. The Japanese Warrior in *Konjaku Monogatari*', in *Monumenta Nipponica*, vol. 28, no. 2
Yamada, Nakaba. *Ghenkō, the Mongol Invasion of Japan*. London, 1916
Yamada, Jirōkichi. *Nihon Kendō-shi*. Tokyo, 1960
Yuasa, Jōzan. *Jōzan Kidan*. Tokyo, 1965

Index and Glossary

INDEX

INDEX